Social Anthropology

Investigating Human Social Life

Second Edition

D0306288

Professor Alan Barnard

Professor of the Anthropology of Southern Africa
University of Edinburgh

www.studymates.co.uk

First published by Studymates Limited, PO Box 225, PO Box 225, Abergele, Conwy County LL18 9AY, U.K.

Second edition 2006

© 2000 and 2006 by Alan Barnard

ISBN-10: 1-84285-084-9
ISBN-13: 9781842 850 848

Typeset by PDQ Typesetting, Newcastle-under-Lyme
Printed and bound by Baskerville Press

Contents

Foreword

Social anthropology is a very odd subject, for three reasons. First, it is hard to say what it is the study *of*; secondly, it is not at all clear what you have to *do* to study it; and thirdly, no-one seems to know how to tell the difference between *studying* anthropology and practising it. For the student encountering the subject for the first time, these questions can be disconcerting, to say the least. By saying a few words about each, I hope to put Alan Barnard's practical introduction in perspective, and to show why it is such an invaluable resource, for both students and teachers of anthropology.

It would be easy to say that social anthropology is the study of human societies – not just our own society but all societies, everywhere. But this only begs further questions. You can see and touch a fellow human being, but have you ever seen or touched a society? Evidently, societies don't exist for anthropologists in quite the same way that rocks exist for geologists, or living organisms for biologists. We think we live in societies, but can anyone ever tell where his or her society ends, and another one begins? The problem of drawing boundaries around a society seems as insoluble as that of demarcating periods of history. Human life goes on, in time and across space, regardless of how we try to divide it up. Granted that we're not sure what societies are, or even whether they exist at all, couldn't we simply say that anthropology is the study of people? There is a lot to be said for this view, but it doesn't help us to distinguish anthropology from all the other academic disciplines that claim to deal with people in one way or another, from history and psychology to the various branches of human biology and biomedicine. What is special about anthropology, I think, is that we don't so much study people as study *with* people. We learn how to see things (or hear them, or touch them) in the ways they do. And that can lead us to perceive our own world quite differently too. In a way, then, an education in anthropology does not furnish us with knowledge *about* the world – about people and their societies. More than that, it educates our *perception* of the world, and opens our eyes to other possibilities of being. It is about learning how to learn.

For just this reason, however, anthropology is a subject without any firmly established body of knowledge that the teacher might hope to pass on and the student to assimilate. Anyone who expects to be served up with such knowledge is bound to be disappointed. Precisely because anthropology is a way of studying *with* people, rather than simply the study *of* people, there are few proper textbooks on the subject, and those that do exist are little used in teaching. One of the things that anthropological research has shown, time and again, is that people are not like containers that are simply 'filled up' with information peculiar to their cultural tradition, but are rather active participants in a process in which knowledge is forever being created or discovered anew. If this is the way people learn in any society, then it must also be true of the way students learn in our own. Thus the student is not so much a recipient of authorised knowledge issuing from a superior source in the academy, as a co-participant and co-discoverer in the shared pursuit of human understanding. But in order to be able to participate in this pursuit, you need to do two things. First, you need to enter into a dialogue with others who have experiences and understandings to share. You can engage in this dialogue directly with your teachers and student colleagues, and indirectly with other anthropologists, through their writings. Secondly, you need to provide yourself with a set of signposts to help find your way through what, initially, may be pretty unfamiliar terrain. These signposts are precisely what Alan Barnard offers in this indispensable introductory guide. But remember: it is absolutely no substitute for reading, at first-hand, what anthropologists have written on the many themes it covers, or for discussion and debate with fellow students and teachers both in the seminar room and in less formal settings.

Teachers in higher education are continually being told these days, by 'experts' and policy makers who think they know about teaching and learning, that every course should be marked out in advance as a series of steps, with a clear indication of how many steps should have been covered by each stage in the course. The idea is that having completed all the steps, the student should have learned the subject. It is as if teaching and learning were like pouring water into a measuring cylinder. Whatever the merits of such an approach for other subjects, this is not the way anthropology can, or should, be taught. In any course, teachers and students embark together on a shared voyage of discovery. They are explorers. Like any explorers, they have certain goals in mind. While the skills and experience of the teacher are essential in helping to keep the expedition on course, the precise destination is unknown. Indeed how could it be otherwise? The world we live in is not a fixed place but is continually moving on. Being inhabitants of this world, our own endeavours are part of this movement. As the world changes, so do our ideas about it. No teacher can, Canute-like, order the world to stop for just so long as it takes to explain its workings to students. Nor can students ask it to wait until they have passed their examinations.

But if teachers and students are fellow participants in this process of exploration and discovery, what's the difference between studying anthropology and being an anthropologist? None, really. Indeed, one of the great things about studying anthropology is that every student of the subject is already an anthropologist from the very start. And one of the great things about being an anthropologist is that one never ceases to study. It is true that practising anthropologists sometimes say that the essence of what they do lies in fieldwork, in those extended periods of time they spend studying with 'their' people. This sometimes makes students feel that until they can get 'out there' themselves, they are never going to know what anthropology is *really* about. This is a misconception, however. What anthropologists call 'the field' is just some place, somewhere, in this one world that we all inhabit. People can change where they live, they can move about, but they are always living somewhere. So wherever you may live, you're in the field, surrounded by people you know, things you have used, and familiar landscapes. Life is fieldwork, fieldwork is life, and the anthropological problem of understanding other people's understandings is no different, in principle, from the problem that all of us face in our daily lives in relating to the people around us. Yet there is still something special about being an anthropologist. It lies in a certain attitude, which you carry with you wherever you go and bring into whatever you may be doing. The anthropologist is, if you will, continually looking over his or her shoulder, towards the possibility of alternative ways of being. From this 'sideways' perspective, the strange can appear familiar, and the familiar strange. And it's when the anthropologist sits down to write about it that the really difficult work begins!

Social anthropology is not a soft option, not a chance to sit back and listen to weird and wonderful stories about the odd customs of exotic peoples. Intellectually, it is probably among the most challenging disciplines in the entire academic curriculum. It ruthlessly excavates and exposes the preconceptions by means of which we comfortably order our lives, and turns every certainty into a question. This is not a subject for the faint-hearted, but for those who embark in a spirit of adventure, the potential rewards are immense. When you set out, however, make sure to carry a copy of Alan Barnard's introduction in your back pocket. It will undoubtedly come in handy.

Professor Tim Ingold
University of Aberdeen

Author's preface

Worldwide, social anthropology is studied each year by thousands of students, and the field is rapidly growing. Some students will go on to become professional anthropologists. Others will work in related fields: museum work, archaeology, community relations, diplomacy, public administration, journalism and Third World development. Still others will use their knowledge and skills simply as part of their general education.

Whether you intend to make a career of social anthropology or just to study it as an outside subject, this study guide is for you. It is designed to supplement any introductory social anthropology course, and will be useful too for those at intermediate level. It contains the background information you need in order to make the best use of your time. It is full of helpful hints for essays and exams, points for discussion, definitions of technical terms, and summary information. The chapters are organised around the major branches of the subject. They are designed to cover all the basics, including both historical background and contemporary material.

As Tim Ingold writes in his foreword, anthropology is not just a body of knowledge to learn. It is a highly challenging field. The examples and the topics chosen for discussion in this book will help you meet this challenge end encourage you to question what pretty much everyone takes for granted about society. As you enter into debate on the issues presented here, you will yourself learn not only anthropology but also how to think like an anthropologist.

Alan Barnard

alan.barnard@studymates.co.uk

Syllabus checklist

Below is a list of UK institutions which teach social anthropology, either as an Honours degree subject in its own right or as part of a joint degree programme. Similar programmes are available in many other countries (see also Chapter 1). English, Welsh and Northern Irish Honours degrees are normally three years in duration (BA or BSc Honours); Scottish ones are four years (MA Honours). In the latter, social anthropology is widely taught as an outside subject for students doing other degrees. Individual anthropology courses are available at a number of UK colleges and universities in addition to those listed below. Several interdisciplinary courses in the Open University social sciences curriculum also contain material from social anthropology. The information presented here should be correct for 2006 student entry. It is worthwhile to check the websites of relevant universities for up-to-date information for future years, including entry requirements.

The taught masters'-level courses are normally open to students with degrees in other subjects but no prior background in social anthropology. Specialist masters' courses are on offer in a number of universities. Examples include medical anthropology (at several universities), the anthropology of childhood (Brunel), the anthropology of art (University College London), and the anthropology of Japan (Oxford Brookes). See relevant websites or contact the universities themselves for further information on these.

PRE-UNIVERSITY COURSES
International Baccalaureate: Social anthropology taught as distinct subject on the International Baccalaureate syllabus, available at a few schools in the UK and many in other countries

UNDERGRADUATE COURSES
(BA, BSc and MA Honours programmes)
University of Aberdeen: Anthropology available in a single Honours degree and a variety of joint Honours degrees

University of Birmingham: Social anthropology taught as part of degrees in African studies

University of Bristol: Combined degree with archaeology

Brunel University: Combined degrees with communications, psychology, and sociology

University of Cambridge: Honours in archaeology and anthropology; also taught as part of Social and Political Sciences tripos

University of Durham: Single Honours anthropology; joint Honours with archaeology, psychology, and sociology (Durham campus), and health and human sciences (Stockton campus)

University of East London: Single Honours and major, joint or minor subject for example with social research and European studies

University of Edinburgh: Single Honours; joint Honours with Arabic, archaeology, geography, linguistics, social history, social policy, and sociology; also with interdisciplinary development studies, and South Asian studies

University of Glasgow: Social anthropology within the Honours sociology curriculum and in joint degrees

Goldsmiths College (University of London): Honours in anthropology, joint Honours with media, with sociology and with history

University of Hull: Degrees in sociology and social anthropology; sociology, social anthropology and development studies; joint degrees with geography, law, philosophy, politics, gender studies, economic and social history, social policy, and theology

University of Kent at Canterbury: Honours in social anthropology; Honours in anthropology (with other subdisciplines); Honours in medical anthropology; combined Honours with other subjects

University of Liverpool: Social anthropology taught within interdisciplinary centres

London School of Economics and Political Science (University of London): Honours in social anthropology, and with law

University of Manchester: Honours in social anthropology, in combined studies, and joint degrees with comparative religion, linguistics, sociology, etc.

University of Oxford: Honours in archaeology and anthropology and in human sciences

Oxford Brookes University: Honours in anthropology (including biological anthropology); various other degrees with social anthropology modules

The Queen's University of Belfast: Single Honours; joint Honours with archaeology, geography, history, modern languages, music, philosophy, politics and sociology

Roehampton University: Single Honours either in social anthropology or in anthropology (including both biological and social anthropology)

University of St Andrews: Honours in social anthropology; joint Honours with art history, economics, geography, international relations, philosophy, psychology, Scottish history, theology, and various languages

School of Oriental and African Studies (University of London): Honours in social anthropology; joint Honours with art and archaeology, development studies, economics, geography, history, law, linguistics, music, politics, religious studies, and languages

University of Sheffield: Social anthropology modules offered within the sociological studies curriculum

University of Sussex: Anthropology (social anthropology) taught as single Honours and in joint degrees with contemporary European studies, cultural studies, development studies, gender studies, and many other social science subjects, and with languages

University College London (University of London): Honours degrees in anthropology (biological anthropology, social anthropology and material culture), anthropology and geography, and human sciences; joint degrees in anthropology with history and linguistics

University of Wales, Lampeter: Honours in anthropology; integrated degrees in (social) anthropology with archaeology and with religion; social anthropology also taught in with many other subjects as part of the combined Honours programme

University of Wales, Swansea: Honours in (social) anthropology, joint Honours with other subjects

Taught Masters' level conversion courses
(MA, MSc and MRes postgraduate programmes)

University of Aberdeen

University of Birmingham (social anthropology taught within African studies)

University of Bristol

Brunel University

University of Cambridge

University of Durham

University of East Anglia (social anthropology within specialist programmes)

University of East London

University of Edinburgh

University of Glasgow (some social anthropology within sociological studies)

Goldsmiths College (University of London)

University of Hull (social anthropology within applied social sciences)

University of Kent at Canterbury

London School of Economics and Political Science (University of London)

University of Manchester

University of Oxford

Oxford Brookes University

The Queen's University of Belfast

University of St Andrews

School of Oriental and African Studies (University of London)

University of Sussex

University College London (University of London)

University of Wales, Lampeter

Studying Social Anthropology

One-minute overview

Social anthropology is the study of human social life. Students do the subject for a variety of reasons, but most want to learn about the variety and richness of human experience. A knowledge of the similarities and differences between societies can enrich one's understanding of society in general. Social anthropology can supplement the study of many other subjects, and can also be of use in many careers.

In this chapter you will learn:

- what is social anthropology?
- why we study social anthropology?
- about cultural differences
- about human universals
- about social anthropology and other subjects
- about social anthropology and your career

What is social anthropology?

Social anthropology is the study of human social life. The subject is concerned both with diversity and with human universals. It has an interesting history.

Historical background

Social anthropology began in the middle of the 19th century as an intellectual hobby for professional men, especially lawyers. They believed that all societies evolved along similar lines, and that 'primitive' societies held clues to the workings of more 'advanced' societies. They used the data then rapidly becoming available on 'primitive' societies, and speculated on the origins and progress of the family, ritual, religious belief, and politics.

By the 1920s social anthropology had become professional-ised. The first trained anthropologists taught in universities or worked in museums. Instead of relying on the accounts of explorers and missionaries, these anthropologists began to do their own fieldwork. Professionalisation brought with it both new skills in fieldwork and new understandings of human society. Evolution ceased to be the main concern, and the new breed of anthropologists became interested in the day-to-day workings of societies in the present.

Specialisations

Modern anthropologists typically have two specialisations: one regional and the other theoretical. Some have more than one of each.

Regional specialisations
These concern a specific part of the world or a specific group of people. For example:

1. West Africa
2. the Caribbean
3. Amazonia
4. Southeast Asia
5. North Atlantic fishing communities
6. Arctic hunters and reindeer herders
7. Gypsies

Theoretical specialisations
Theoretical specialisations concern an aspect of society, a branch of anthropology, or sometimes a viewpoint or approach to the study of society in general. For example:

1. ethnicity
2. witchcraft
3. gender relations
4. family and kinship
5. economic anthropology
6. applied anthropology
7. Marxism in anthropology

Why study social anthropology?

If you are studying social anthropology, think about what led you into the subject. If you are still undecided, think about the variety of topics the subject includes, and ask yourself which ones are of special interest. Most anthropology students don't aim to become professional anthropologists. They do the subject out of interest or from a desire to use it as background for the pursuit of a more specialised career. Here are some reasons why students do the subject:

1. to gain a wide understanding of society.
2. to learn more about Third World peoples, perhaps with a view to going into a career in social development.
3. to perfect skills in thinking and debating.
4. to supplement a degree in archaeology, psychology, sociology, or whatever.
5. as something completely different!

Figure 1.
Differences can occur within a culture, as here with traditional and modern First People (indigenous Canadian) dress (© David Stafford, 1988; courtesy of David Stafford and Jeanne Cannizzo)
◄

Learning about cultural differences

Many decide to study social anthropology in order to learn about the differences between cultures. Here are some examples.

Greeting people in different cultures

Consider some examples of how people greet each other:

1. In Japan it is customary to bow, whereas in Europe people shake hands when they meet for the first time.
2. In Eastern Europe men hug and kiss each other, whereas in Western Europe they generally don't.
3. In most European countries people shake hands more frequently than they do in the UK.
4. In many European countries, kissing on the cheek or off the cheek is common when greeting between women, or between people of opposite sex. There are different ways of doing this: for example, twice (once just off each cheek) in France, three times in The Netherlands.
5. Within the UK there are similar differences. Men shake hands more frequently than women. Muslims shake hands more frequently than Christians. Hindus greet with the namaste (placing the palms of one's own hands together and bowing), rather than with a handshake.

- *Practise* – greeting people of different cultural background. Note the differences within a social category (men, women, Muslims, Christians, etc.). Then note differences when people of different categories meet. Which form of greeting dominates? Why?

Classifying the world in different cultures

Classifying is part of language, but it is also part of culture. Indeed, many anthropologists argue that learning a culture is like learning a language. Ordinary things, like animals or plants are classified differently in different cultures. A knowledge of this adds to cultural understanding.

Animals may be classified by appearance, activity, or how they rear their young. In many African cultures bats are classified as 'birds' because they are flying animals. In European cultures, influenced by Linnaeus's 18th-century rules of biological taxonomy, bats are classified as 'mammals' because female bats feed their young through their mammary glands.

Similarly, people classify plants by a variety of means. Even within the same society, there may be differences. In Western cookery tomatoes are treated as 'vegetables'. However, in biological science they are 'fruits' because they are the seed-bearing parts of the tomato plant.

As we shall see in chapter 8, there are a variety of ways to classify one's relatives. Terms like 'uncle' and 'aunt' are not universal. In many societies, a person's mother's brother is called by a different term from their father's brother, and is treated quite differently.

Learning about human universals

Differences and similarities are two sides to the same coin. The ultimate case of similarity is that of a cultural, or human universal.

Human universals are modes of thought or behaviour which are the same everywhere. Long ago anthropologists came up with the idea of a psychic unity or psychic identity between all peoples (see also chapter 10). It is not that we humans are all so culturally different that we cannot understand each other. Rather, our cultural differences mask innate similarities in the way we think and act.

Social anthropology helps us to sort out the differences from the universals. For example, languages classify objects differently (bats, uncles, etc.), but all languages are made up of the same basic features (nouns, verbs, sentences, etc.). We can translate ideas from one language to another. We can also translate ideas from one culture to another, because we humans, at a fundamental level, are all the same.

Those anthropologists who emphasise cultural differences are called relativists. Anti-relativists reject that emphasis and concentrate instead on either similarities or human universals.

Question – Does this mean that anthropology is polarised between two radically different viewpoints?

Answer – Yes, and no. It is a truism that cultures are both different from each other and somehow all similar. While some anthropologists may hold radically relativist or anti-relativist positions, most fall in between. One's theoretical position does, in fact, depend on the specific question one is trying to answer. Examples of this will become apparent throughout this book.

Social anthropology and other subjects

The 'four fields' approach

There are several ways in which the subject matter of social anthropology combines with other disciplines. The issue of relativism is one of concern to philosophy, that of psychic unity, to psychology. Another grouping of disciplines considers social anthropology as a whole to be part of a broadly-conceived anthropological science, made up of four distinct parts.

This 'four-fields' approach is the basic one in several countries, notably the US and Canada. It has its influence in the UK too, though rarely with all four of the 'four fields' being taught in the same department.

The 'four fields' are:

1. *Physical or biological anthropology*
'Physical anthropology' is the older term and the one still more common in North America. 'Biological anthropology' is heard more often in the UK today, and is more accurate since the field includes not only comparative anatomy ('physical' aspects of being human) but also genetics, demography, etc. This field also covers topics like human biological evolution and biological differences between human populations.

2. *Prehistoric archaeology*
The study of the remains of past civilisations, including cultures in direct continuity with those of living ones (for example, Native North Americans or Australian Aborigines).

3. *Anthropological linguistics*
A branch of both linguistics and anthropology. It concentrates on differences between languages, and often relates aspects of language to aspects of culture. It includes the way people classify plants, animals, and so on, as well as aspects of grammar.

4. *Cultural or social anthropology*
'Cultural anthropology' is the term in common use in North America, while 'social anthropology' is more common in the UK and elsewhere. They mean roughly the same thing. Historically, there has been a slight propensity for American anthropologists to talk more about cultural differences and British anthropologists to talk more about different societies. However, this is no longer as true as it once was.

Question – So, what is the natural place of social anthropology as a branch of knowledge?

Answer – Social anthropology has no such natural place. Like its subject matter, social anthropology is conditional on cultural context – the cultural context of university administration, as well as the historical context in which it emerged in different countries.

Social anthropology and the social sciences

A social science is a field of study whose object is understanding some aspect of society. Sociology, psychology, political science, economics, and at least certain branches of geography, education and history (as well as anthropology) qualify as social sciences.

If you are studying one or more other social sciences, see if you can think of link-ups between social anthropology and your other courses.

1. Sociology and social anthropology are both concerned with the study of society in the abstract. Among the differences between them, social anthropology emphasises cultural difference and therefore implies more of a comparative or cross-cultural perspective.

2. Psychology includes the study of child-rearing and the relation between culture and personality. So does social anthropology.

3. Political science involves the study of power relations, also an important topic in anthropology.

4. Economics has a claim to being the first social science (dating from the 18th century). In some universities there are introductory courses which aim to look at common features between social sciences as diverse as economics and social anthropology.

5. Geography and social anthropology both include the study of settlement patterns and culture contact. Cultural ecology is a related field, often treated as part of social anthropology. And of course both geography and social anthropology imply 'area studies' interests (for example sub-Saharan Africa or South Asia).

6. Education has links, too, especially multi-cultural education and the comparative study of educational systems.

7. History also has links, especially economic and social history. The difference is that history is essentially diachronic (looking at things through time), whereas most anthropologists prefer a synchronic approach (looking at things at one point in time).

8. Related arts subjects are also relevant, especially in regard to the social aspects. These subjects include art history and more generally the study of the visual arts (such as painting, sculpture and decoration) and the performing arts (such as drama, music and dance). These of course differ from society to society.

Figure 2. Traditional dancing in Zimbabwe (© Joost Fontein, 1997) ▼

UK degree programmes

In the UK there are well over a hundred degree programmes that include social anthropology as either the major component or one of two major components. These fall broadly into six categories.

1. Degrees in social anthropology (single Honours).

2. Joint or combined degrees in social anthropology and another subject, usually but not always a social science.

3. Degrees in general anthropology (similar to the 'four fields'

model, though usually excluding linguistics).

4. Degrees in social anthropology with an interdisciplinary field (for example social anthropology with gender studies).

5. Degrees with social anthropology as a second main subject within another degree programme (typically sociology with social anthropology).

6. Specialised anthropology degrees (for example medical anthropology, usually taught at postgraduate level).

Social anthropology and your career

Social anthropology is appropriate for many careers. Here are just a few suggestions (some requiring further career training):

museum work
librarianship
research work of many kinds
social work
charity organisation
charity work abroad
tourism

teaching
health care
civil service
diplomatic service
journalism and the media
politics

Social anthropology graduates have included several princes and at least one president, many top civil servants and directors of charities, several ambassadors from various countries, a well-known television journalist, and a British cabinet minister. Early anthropologists came into the discipline from fields such as medicine, the law, and the church. Today, quite a few graduates go in the opposite direction, combining a first degree in anthropology with further qualifications to join such traditional professions.

Tutorial

Progress questions

1 Name some differences between cultures. Name some similarities.

2 How does social anthropology relate to other subjects?

3 What are the career possibilities of a social anthropology graduate?

Seminar discussion

1 Is cultural difference necessarily divisive? Or can a shared understanding of cultural difference create a bond between those of diverse origin?

2 Why do you think social anthropology is linked with different subjects in such different ways?

Practical assignment

Discuss with your classmates, friends or relatives how cultural differences might have affected them. Think about your own experiences when on holiday abroad or in dealing with people from a different background. Then write down your thoughts. (Treat this as your first exercise in anthropological fieldwork.)

Study, revision and exam tips

1 Consider what you hope to get out of your course. Remember, only a minority of university subjects (like dentistry, medicine, law, social work, divinity) are directly related to careers. The rest (like philosophy, history, literature, social anthropology) are taken mainly for their value in one's general education.

2 Remember that the term 'anthropology' is often heard as a shorthand way of saying 'social anthropology'. Take care how you use it, and be aware that 'anthropology' (especially in North American writings) can refer to the wider subject containing all 'four fields'.

3 When choosing optional courses, consider both how they might build on your previous courses and how they might be useful in your intended career.

2 **Ethnography: Writing About Peoples**

One-minute overview

Ethnography means writing about peoples. The object of ethnography is to get inside another culture, and ultimately to compare the results to ethnographic studies of other cultures. The tradition of doing ethnography dates from the 19th century, and anthropology students still study classic ethnographies (mainly from the early 20th century). Ethnography today is based on a refinement of the early 20th-century example. In this chapter you will cover:

- appreciating classic ethnographies
- understanding the structure of an ethnography
- reading recent ethnographies
- getting inside another culture
- using ethnography in your essays and exams

Appreciating classic ethnographies

While the literal meaning of ethnography is 'writing about peoples', anthropologists use the word in two ways. On the one hand it refers to doing fieldwork and taking notes. On the other, it refers to the practice of writing or to the finished writings themselves. Chances are you will have to read some classic ethnographies in your course. Try to think of them not just as old but as classics. The great ethnographers often made contributions to theoretical ideas through their ethnography.

Three famous ethnographers

Boas

Franz Boas (1858–1942) was a German-American anthropologist originally trained in physics and geography. He studied the Inuit or Eskimo of Baffin Island and Kwakiutl of British Columbia.

Boas published hundreds of journal articles but relatively few books. For most of his career he was based at Columbia University in New York, where he trained generations of American students in ethnographic method. His ethnographies include:

> *The Central Eskimo* (1888)
> *The Social Organization and Secret Societies of the Kwakiutl Indians* (1897)
> *The Religion of the Kwakiutl Indians* (1930)
> *Kwakiutl Culture as Reflected in Mythology* (1935)

Compilations include *Kwakiutl Ethnography* (edited by Helen Codere, 1967).

1. Regarded as the founder of modern American anthropology.
2. Emphasised practising local activities.
3. Also emphasised the use of the native language and the recording of minute details of culture.

Figure 3. Franz Boas, ca. 1940
▶

Malinowski

Bronislaw Malinowski (1884–1942) was a Polish-British anthropologist originally trained in mathematics, physics and philosophy. He studied the Trobriand Islanders of Papua New Guinea. His main interests were economics, kinship, and the relation between individual and society. At the height of his career he was based at London School of Economics, where he trained the first generation of professional British anthropologists. His Trobriand ethnographies include:

Argonauts of the Western Pacific (1922)
Crime and Custom in Savage Society (1926)
Sex and Repression in Savage Society (1927)
The Sexual Life of Savages in Northwestern Melanesia (1929)
Coral Gardens and Their Magic (1935)

Also of interest is his posthumously-published fieldwork diary *A Diary in the Strict Sense of the Term* (1967), and the compilation *The Ethnography of Malinowski* (edited by Michael Young, 1979).

1. Regarded as one of the two founders of modern British anthropology (the other is A.R. Radcliffe-Brown, discussed in chapter 10).
2. Emphasised participant-observation, the use of the native language, and the functions of social institutions in relation to the individual.

Figure 4.
Bronislaw
Malinowski in
silhouette inside
his tent,
Trobriand
Islands, 1918
◄

Evans-Pritchard

E.E. Evans-Pritchard (1902–1973) was a British anthropologist originally trained in history. He studied Azande and Nuer in Sudan, and other East African groups. His interests included belief systems, politics, and kinship. Evans-Pritchard taught at Oxford University and was knighted in 1971. His main ethnographies are:

> *Witchcraft, Oracles and Magic among the Azande* (1937; abridged edition 1976)
> *The Nuer* (1940)
> *The Sanusi of Cyrenaica* (1949)
> *Kinship and Marriage among the Nuer* (1951)
> *Nuer Religion* (1956)
> *The Azande* (1971)
> *Man and Woman among the Azande* (1974)

Witchcraft, Oracles and Magic remains a classic study of 'primitive thought' (see chapter 6).

1. His early Nuer works were diverse in topic but mainly in the Malinowskian tradition.
2. However, with Nuer Religion he turned against an interest in how society works (functionalism) towards one in how people see their world (interpretivism).

Figure 5.
E. E. Evans-Pritchard with Zande (Azande), ca. 1928 ▶

Question – Why is it important to know about old ethnographies?

Answer – Debates between anthropologists are often played out through examples they all know – the ones from the classic ethnographies. Lecturers use these classics in introductory teaching too, as they tend to be freer of jargon than more recent ethnographies. Ethnographers like Boas, Malinowski and Evans-Pritchard made discoveries and presented arguments about human society which are still talked about.

Understanding the structure of an ethnography

When you read an ethnography, think about its structure. Often this will help you to understand the author's approach and follow what he or she is trying to say. Some examples are shown in figure 6.

Figure 6. Typical structures of ethno-graphies ◄

Ethnography with a seamless narrative
1. the environment of the people
2. village life
3. the household
4. family and kinship
5. sex and marriage
6. youth and old age
7. rituals of life and death

Ethnography structured on the life cycle
1. doing fieldwork with the people
2. birth and the naming ceremony
3. growing up
4. initiation and marriage
5. adulthood and raising children
6. old age
7. death and funerals

> **Ethnography structured on social systems**
> 1. history of the people
> 2. economic activities
> 3. political relations
> 4. law and social control
> 5. the kinship system
> 6. ritual and belief
> 7. social change

Ethnographies with a seamless narrative

The ethnographies published between the first and second world wars are generally long. Many are poorly organised. However, they can be a pleasure to read. Their authors often tried to weave the details of social life into a seamless narrative. A good example is the Polynesian ethnography *We The Tikopia* (1936), by Malinowski's student Sir Raymond Firth. The main text is 599 pages, each page and each chapter connected to the next, but with no major breaks by topic.

Consider these points in reference to the first hypothetical ethnography of figure 6.

(a) The chapter on the environment sets the scene.

(b) The chapters are ordered roughly from general to specific themes.

(c) The theme of each succeeding chapter is related to the previous one, but the themes do not parallel each other: some concern the life cycle and others concern social systems.

Ethnographies structured on the life cycle

Another method is to emphasise the life cycle – from childhood to old age. One example is the Australian ethnography *Aboriginal Woman* (1939), by Phyllis Kaberry, another of Malinowski's students. She alternates between the sacred and the profane (secular) aspects of each period of life for the women of the Kimberleys (in Western Australia). Other examples are Marjorie Shostak's Nisa: *The Life and Words of a !Kung Woman* (1981) and Lila Abu-Lughod's *Writing Women's Worlds: Bedouin Stories* (1993). These focus on women's lives, both in relation to men and in relation to other women.

Consider these points in reference to the second hypothetical ethnography:

(a) It begins with an overview of the fieldwork itself. Such a personal touch is most typically associated with ethnographies which present a culture through the eyes of individuals.

(b) There is an emphasis on activities, notably activities related to age. Often this kind of ethnography emphasises gender distinctions too, as activities often vary according to gender.

Ethnographies structured on social systems

It is common for ethnographies to be structured around the idea of social systems. Evans-Pritchard's ethnographies are examples. This structure is also found as the basis of short, student-friendly monographs like Robert Tonkinson's *The Mardudjara Aborigines* (second edition, 1991) or Richard Lee's *The Dobe Ju/'hoansi* (third edition, 2003).

Consider these points in reference to the third hypothetical ethnography.

(a) It begins with a chapter on history (the past) and concludes with a chapter on social change (pointing towards the future). This is typical where there is a presumption of social stability in the rest of the book.

(b) The middle chapters are ordered from the concrete (economic activities) to the more abstract (ritual and belief).

The presumption of social stability is related to the concept of the ethnographic present. This means the time of the fieldwork, and anthropologists frequently refer to happenings in other cultures in the present tense even when the time of fieldwork was long ago.

Reading recent ethnographies

Most recent ethnographies concern specific themes – economic activities, political power, rituals of birth, initiation, marriage, death, etc. They do not aim to cover everything.

Watching for theoretical and stylistic indicators

Ethnographies are not written in a theoretical vacuum. The ethnographer's theoretical position will come through. See what presuppositions or prior interests the writer has.

For example

(a) Is the ethnographer mainly interested in showing how everything fits together?

(b) Or is he interested in explaining how people in the society view their world?

Look also for stylistic indicators

(a) Does the account read like a scientific text, or more like a story?

(b) How does the ethnographer portray the individuals she writes about?

(c) Are they exemplars of social behaviour, or do they come alive as real people?

Many anthropologists today believe it is better if ethnographies portray individuals more as characters in fiction than as units of social structure. Abu-Lughod's *Writing Women's Worlds* (mentioned above) is a good example.

Reflexivity: finding the ethnographer in the ethnography

Another characteristic of recent ethnography is the emphasis on reflexivity: the ethnographer reflecting on her role as ethnographer. Increasingly, ethnographers are more subjective, regarding ethnography less as an objective account of an alien society and more as an attempt to bridge the divide between cultures. Reflexivity today is more than an activity undertaken during fieldwork. It is also a style of writing. Reflexive ethnographers put themselves into the picture.

While anthropologists welcomed the notion of reflexivity when it became popular in the 1980s, it has disadvantages as well as advantages.

Advantages of reflexivity

1. Being aware of possible biases introduced by the ethnographer

2. Expressing findings with due modesty (not 'The Bongo believe X is true', but 'Bongo told me that . . .')

Disadvantages of reflexivity

1. An inability to make firm, objective statements about the society or culture

2. An overemphasis on the ethnographer, rather than the people

Getting inside another culture

Anthropologists have long debated the degree to which an ethnographer can or should try to get inside another culture. Essentially there are three views:

1. Our task is to understand society from the outside. We should be objective. This approach is called **functionalist** and derived from the work of Malinowski.

2. We should learn to 'think like a native' – to feel and understand the world as they do. This approach is **interpretivist**, in the spirit of Evans-Pritchard.

3. The interpretation or translation of culture is an elusive ideal. We can strive for it, but we can never quite achieve it. We should instead think of a dialogue between cultures. This approach is also **interpretivist** but associated more with Clifford Geertz (see chapter 10). Its more radical adherents call themselves postmodernists. Rejecting the notion of a single scientific truth, they tend to emphasise the fieldwork experience for the fieldworker over the results of the fieldwork itself.

Question – If, as some argue, it is not really possible to 'get inside' another culture then why should we try?

Answer – This is a philosophical question, but probably most anthropologists would say we should try because some understanding is better than none. The very process of trying yields insights.

Question – How do I know which viewpoint is best? I do not have enough knowledge of ethnography to make a judgement.

Answer – No amount of evidence, by itself, will provide the answer to questions like whether it is possible to get inside another culture. It is to some extent a matter of opinion. In your essays and exams you are being assessed according to your ability to argue a good case, not for having the correct answer.

Comparing cultural differences

Purposes

In a way, comparison is the opposite of getting inside another culture. Its purposes are:

1. to highlight what is important or interesting in one culture by seeing it through the eyes of another

2. to account for differences between cultures in a systematic way

Anthropological comparison

Anthropological comparison falls into three general styles:

1. *Illustrative comparison*
This kind of comparison involves description. The emphasis is on highlighting some aspect of culture. For example, we might choose an example of a culture in which men are dominant and compare it to one in which men and women are more equal.

2. *Controlled comparison*
Here we are trying to explain something by narrowing the range of variables, in the way chemists or physicists might. We might look at several closely-related societies to see how differences in one aspect of culture might affect other aspects.

3. *Global comparison*
This form of comparison takes a large sample – from all over a region, from all societies of a certain type (such as hunter-gatherers), or all over the world indiscriminately. It aims at comprehensiveness, though at the expense of clarity and control.

Question – Is comparison really that important? Why can we not just read ethnographies and enjoy them?

Answer – Of course you can just read ethnographies to enjoy them. Some of the earliest were written for this purpose. However, ethnographies also exist as source material for comparative studies. Through comparison, anthropologists can answer questions like how peoples are related, the extent to which certain phenomena are natural or cultural (for example, the incest taboo), or how changes in environment or technology affect society.

One of the main purposes of ethnography is to provide the building blocks for larger anthropological problems like these. Without ethnography, there can be no anthropology. But without comparison, ethnography loses its power to explain.

Using ethnography in your essays and exams

It is almost always an advantage to use ethnography in your essays and exams. But there are right and wrong ways of doing it.

Using ethnography well

To use ethnography well:

1. Locate important information, but discard what you don't need. Systematise what you use.

2. Think carefully about the appropriate number of examples for your essay or class presentation. More is not necessarily better.

3. Use contrasting or complementary examples.

4. Compare your examples. Don't just present them.

Example

Imagine your tutor has set an essay:

'Discuss the importance of fishing in Melanesian society.'

One way of handling it would be to concentrate on a few good ethnographies and look for similarities and differences in the relative importance of fishing. You might concentrate on a couple of coastal societies where fishing is the main occupation, and perhaps contrast these to an inland society where there is little or no fishing. You might look for relations between fishing and trade. Do the coastal societies trade for tools when they make fishing voyages? Do the inland people trade other goods for fish? An essay addressing such questions might usefully employ elements of both illustrative and controlled comparison.

On the other hand, you might want to cover a larger sample of all the Melanesian fishing societies. A word of warning: if you throw your net too wide, you may end up saying too little about your examples. If you go for more than three or four, it is probably best to systematise the information you gather in order to come up with useful generalisations. Otherwise, stick to a smaller number of good examples to support your argument.

Tutorial

Progress questions

1 How has ethnography changed through time?

2 Why is ethnography not just a matter of recording facts?

3 How does ethnography relate to comparison?

Seminar discussion questions

1 Do you think classic ethnographies have as much to teach us as recent ones?

2 What is the best way to structure an ethnographic report?

Practical assignment

Imagine you are a professional anthropologist planning an ethnographic study. Pick a topic and a location. Design an ethnographic study of a year's duration. Use the internet to find sources of funding, immigration and medical requirements, names of anthropologists who have worked in the location before, a relevant bibliography, and possibilities for publishing your results.

Study, revision and exam tips

1 Read old as well as recent ethnographies, but be aware of the time periods to which they refer. Remember the date a book is published; it may be significant to refer to it in an essay or exam.

2   Pay attention to the structure of a monograph. Think why it might be organised the way it is.

3   In both your reading and your writing, concentrate on what you need answer the question set. You may need to read only twenty pages of a 400-page ethnography to do this! Use the contents and indexes to locate what you want.

3 Ecology: Understanding Environment and Technology

One-minute overview

Ecology is the study of relations between living organisms in an environment. In anthropology, it refers to relations between people in their environment and how they use technology to utilise that environment. Ecological anthropologists concentrate on how people make a living and often specialise in the study of specific kinds of society on this basis: hunting-and-gathering societies, fishing societies, etc. In this chapter you will cover:

■ how environment influences society
■ technology as a social force
■ making a living
■ ecology and globalisation

How environment influences society

Those who specialise in the study of relations between environment and society are called ecological anthropologists. They call their subject either ecological anthropology, cultural ecology or social ecology.

Debating the relation between environment and society

There is much debate about the influence of environment on society.

1.   Some anthropologists argue that environment determines social organisation, at least for those societies which rely heavily on simple technology.

2. Many more argue that the environment merely limits how society develops.

3. Still others argue that there is only a loose relation between environment and society.

Most cultural ecologists hold the middle view. They argue that social organisation is formed by a combination of environmental influence and the specific cultural history of a people.

Figure 7. Making a living in the beautiful but harsh environment of northern Namibia (© Alan Barnard, 1991)▼

Examples of environmental influence

1. Living where water supplies are scant will limit the size of groups. Desert areas such as the Sahara or the Kalahari tend to have small and dispersed populations, or populations concentrated around meagre water resources.

2. Places with varying resources tend to be ideal for peoples on the move or peoples wishing to trade. As we shall see in the next chapter, Native North Americans of the north west coast used to move within their territories in search of the best fishing and food-gathering grounds. When one group acquired more

resources than others, they would give them away in
ceremonies which conferred prestige on the givers.

3. Climates with extreme seasonal variation tend to be
    conducive to social organisations with seasonal diversity.
    As we shall see later in this chapter, Inuit of Arctic
    North America have very different activities in summer
    and winter.

Key concepts in ecological anthropology

Ecological anthropologists use a number of concepts which
you should become familiar with.

1. **Adaptation** refers to the ability of a people to respond
    favourably to environmental stress.

2. A **means of subsistence** is a method of obtaining a
    living from the environment. These include hunting,
    gathering, fishing, herding livestock, and agriculture (of
    various kinds).

3. An **ecological niche** is a set of resources utilised by a
    particular group in an environment. Sometimes
    different groups (say, hunters and herders) will exploit
    different niches in the same environment.

4. The **carrying capacity** is the maximum number of
    people who can live in a given environment. Sometimes
    this supposes a specific means of subsistence.

5. **Social organisation** refers to the activities of members
    of a society. It is related to the idea of society as social
    structure (the positions people occupy in relation to
    one another).

6. **Cultural materialism** is the extreme view that
    environment and technology together determine the
    social organisation. Its leading proponent was American
    anthropologist Marvin Harris (1927–2001), and the key
    text is his 1979 book entitled *Cultural Materialism*.

Question – How can ecological anthropologists tell whether it really is the environment or just historical accident which creates social organisation?

Answer – Chances are, it is a bit of both. However, ecological anthropologists are by definition interested in relations between environment and social organisation. They infer influence through analysis of one society or through comparison of two closely-related societies.

Question – How did anthropologists first come to be interested in questions like this?

Answer – Ecological anthropology is usually dated to the publication of *Theory of Culture Change* (1955), by American anthropologist Julian H. Steward (1902-1972). Ethnographers, especially those working in hunting-and-gathering societies, had long noticed that environment was important. What Steward did was to put together examples of how environment and technology affect social organisation, compare these in an evolutionary framework, and encourage his students to do studies focusing on these things.

Question – What about more recent developments? What's the latest?

Answer – Ecological anthropologists today are frequently more interested in how ordinary people view their environments. Again, hunter-gatherers are the key. In several articles beginning with one in *Current Anthropology* in 1990, Israeli anthropologist Nurit Bird-David has argued that hunter-gatherers see themselves as living in 'giving environments', ones which provide plentiful resources to those who know how to use them.

Technology as a social force

Irrigation in the ancient Near East

Agriculture is practised in virtually every part of the world, but the technology differs. Early farmers in ancient Mesopotamia and Egypt made use of the natural seasonal cycles of the rise and fall of water levels along great perennial rivers. Later they developed irrigation systems which involved bringing water into previously dry lands. This enabled an increase in population and led ultimately to urbanism. As cities were formed along the banks of rivers, flood control became important. This required an increase in labour and new organisational forms for that labour. Eventually, it is suggested, social hierarchies developed, with aristocratic and priestly classes at the top and slaves at the bottom.

This pattern was argued most strongly by German-American historian Karl A. Wittfogel in his book *Oriental Despotism* (1957). Wittfogel believed that China, India, and the ancient civilisations of South and Central America developed in a similar way, with a close relation between irrigation, intensive food-production, urbanisation, social stratification, and the rise of the state as a political institution.

However, American anthropologist Robert McCormick Adams has argued, mainly on the basis of archaeological evidence, against Wittfogel's premise that irrigation technology leads to urbanisation and complex political structures. His view is that urbanisation preceded complex political structures and technological improvements such as advanced irrigation systems.

The introduction of the horse on the Great Plains

Native North Americans acquired horses from Spaniards as early as the sixteenth century, and by the eighteenth century all the groups of the Great Plains had them: Blackfoot,

Sioux, Cheyenne, Comanche, Crow, etc. The ability to ride and hunt from horseback was, in a very real sense, a technological innovation, and it led directly to changes in social organisation.

Before the coming of the horse, Plains peoples were mainly settled cultivators who lived peaceably with their neighbours. After the horse, they took to a nomadic way of life and to hunting buffalo. Raiding and warfare spread, and so too did social values and religious ideas based on individual glory and spiritual power through killing. Eventually, larger tribal groupings emerged for the protection of families, as well as for warfare.

Clearly the horse was a cause of social change in this case. However, peoples in other parts of the world acquired horses and skills in riding without the same consequences.

Making a living

Hunters and gatherers

Hunting-and-gathering peoples are those who subsist predominantly by hunting and gathering. Some anthropologists reserve the term for those who subsist exclusively by hunting and gathering, or for those who hunt, gather and fish and have no livestock or agriculture. Hunting, gathering and fishing were the sole means of subsistence for the whole of humankind just 12,000 years ago. Today, there are virtually no 'pure' hunter-gatherers left.

However, many peoples retain a pride in their hunting-and-gathering past, and many still subsist partly by these means. Peoples generally considered hunter-gatherers include, by continent:

- *Africa* – Bushmen or San (actually several different peoples of Southern Africa; see figure 8), Pygmies (likewise various forest-dwelling peoples of Central Africa), and Hadza (East Africa)

Figure 8.
*!Xõo Bushman
hunter-gatherers
(© Alan
Barnard, 1982)*

- *Asia* – Ket and Yukaghir (Siberia), Andaman Islanders, and a number of small groups of India, Southeast Asia and the Philippines

- *Australia* – Aborigines throughout the continent

- *North America* – Inuit or Eskimo, Algonkians (including Cree), Northern Athapaskans, and several smaller groups

- *South America* – Ona and Yahgan (Tierra del Fuego), and a few Amazonian groups

Hunting-and-gathering societies have long been of interest to ecological anthropologists because of their close relation to the environments they inhabit. Julian Steward, founder of ecological anthropology, specialised in the study of the remnant hunter-gatherers of California and other parts of the Americas. Yet even before Steward, hunter-gatherers attracted attention.

One pioneering study of continuing relevance is a literature survey by French anthropologist Marcel Mauss (1872-1950). First published in French in 1904-05, it appeared in English as *Seasonal Variations of the Eskimo* in 1979. Mauss's special concern was the strict seasonal difference between summer and winter in northern Canada (see figure 9).

Some Inuit inhabit two winter houses:

1. a private house (which could be wooden or, in Canada, a snow house or igdlu)

2. a collective house called a kashim or a 'place of assembly'. This is a large house with room for the entire population of a settlement.

Shamans would perform rituals to purify the group against the violation of taboos. There would be public confessions, trance performances, ceremonial lighting and extinguishing of fires, and even communal sex. The summer was the opposite. Each Inuit family would leave the communal area in order to hunt and fish in their own territories. Traditional ceremonies there were concerned with hunting.

summer	winter
dispersal of families on the land	aggregation of larger groups
individual activities dominate	collective activities dominate
hunting the main economic pursuit	fishing the main economic pursuit
rituals of human/animal communication	rituals of human relations

Figure 9. Inuit seasons ▶

More generally, attributes of hunting-and-gathering societies include:

1. seasonal migrations or nomadic movements within group territories

2. large territories for the size of population

3. flexibility in group structure

4. political and economic equality

5. some gender specialisation (men hunt and women gather)

6. widespread sharing of goods within the community

Fishing

Many hunter-gatherers also fish, but sometimes a distinction is made between these societies and those who are relatively sedentary and traditionally well-off because of their fishing activities. Relatively sedentary fishing-hunting-gathering societies include:

Figure 10. Australian Aborigines fishing for crabs (© Alan Barnard, 1988)
▼

- *Asia* – Ainu (Japan)

- *North America* – Kwakiutl and other north west coast groups

Herding

Herders or pastoralists represent another kind of society. Peoples generally considered pastoralists include:

- *Africa* – Tuareg (North Africa), Fulani (West Africa), Nuer, Maasai and many other peoples (East Africa), Nama, Herero and other groups (Southern Africa)

- *Asia* – Mongols, Tibetans and many other groups

- *Europe* – Saami or Lapps (reindeer herders of the far north)

- *South America* – some isolated Andean groups

Some pastoralists are almost totally dependent on their livestock. The Maasai of Kenya and Tanzania are a good example.

Others are less so, but nevertheless depend on their livestock for their social identity while exploiting a complex of resources in their environment. Evans-Pritchard's famous study *The Nuer* (1940) is the classic one of such a people (see also chapter 2). The Nuer of Sudan exploit different resources, including fish and agricultural goods, seasonally. They take their cattle with them from upland villages to large lowland camps as the waters recede in the annual cycle (the rainy season is roughly May to November, and the dry season, December to April). This is shown in figure 11.

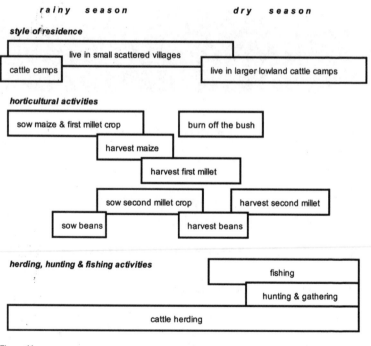

Figure 11.
Nuer seasonal
activities ▲

General attributes of herding societies are broadly similar to those of hunting-and-gathering societies:

1. seasonal migrations or nomadic movements, sometimes without regard to territory
2. large territories for the size of population
3. political and economic equality
4. sharp gender division (generally, only men and boys herd animals)

Agriculture

Agriculture may be defined in various ways, but it is useful here to distinguish two basic types: small-scale horticulture and large-scale, advanced agriculture.

Small-scale horticulturists include:

- *Africa* – most peoples on the continent

- *Asia* – most of the inhabitants of South and Southeast Asia, as well as Papua New Guinea

- *Europe* – some peasant communities in Southern Europe

- *North America* – Ojibwa and other groups (northeast); Hopi, Navaho and others (southwest)

- *South America* – the great majority of Amazonian peoples

Characteristics of these societies are:

1. an emphasis on vegetable production (often with some livestock or fishing)
2. slash-and-burn methods of cultivation (brush is burned off and fields left fallow)
3. mechanisms for redistribution of wealth (e.g. by chiefs)
4. otherwise, relative political and economic equality
5. some gender differentiation in economic activities

Advanced agriculure

Advanced agricultural peoples today cover most of the

world. While the origins of such agricultural systems are of interest, these tend to be more appropriately thought of within archaeology and political anthropology rather than ecological anthropology. This is largely because of their importance in defining the origins of state political entities. Such societies include:

- *Africa* – Egypt since ancient times
- *Asia* – ancient civilisations of Mesopotamia, China, etc.
- *Europe* – much of Europe over the last few centuries
- *North America* – ancient Aztecs (Mexico)
- *South America* – ancient Incas (Peru)

Characteristics of these societies are:

1. an emphasis on grain production
2. irrigation
3. complex political structures
4. great social differentiation (with non-producing as well as producing classes)
5. great social inequalities

Manufacturing and trading

Peoples engaged heavily in manufacturing and trade include:

- *Africa* – Arab traders in East Africa, Hausa and others in West Africa, modern oil and mineral producers in several parts of the continent
- *Asia* – ancient and modern societies, especially today in East and Southeast Asia
- *Australia* – modern Australia
- *Europe* – modern Europe
- *North America* – modern North America
- *South America* – modern South America

Most of these societies are similar in their characteristics to advanced agricultural societies.

Ecology and globalisation

The spread of advanced technology, the production of 'greenhouse gasses', the destruction of rainforests, and the reduction in the number of species worldwide, have all led to a growing interest in the global environment.

Two contributions social anthropology has to make are:

1. providing basic data on traditional uses of the environment.
2. providing a basis for comparison through in-depth ethnographic studies of environmental use.

There will also be more specific contributions related to how particular societies can be expected to adapt in the face of globalisation.

One tendency has been the coming together of economic systems. All economies are now connected through trade. Another has been the tendency of cultures to become more like each other, meaning less diversity than had previously been the case. The lack of diversity becomes important with regard to environmental knowledge, which may be quite specific.

Figure 12. Globalisation: market in California with vegetables from around the world (© Alan Barnard, 2002)

▼

Indigenous inhabitants of the Amazonian rainforests, for example, know their unique environments very well. Studies such as Philippe Descola's *The Spears of Twilight* (on life and death in the Amazon jungle, 1993) show both the detailed environmental knowledge such peoples have and how it is different from the understandings of peoples in the West. While ecologists proper are concerned with bio-diversity, ecological anthropologists can contribute through helping the outside world to become aware of the indigenous knowledge of local environments.

Tutorial

Progress questions

1. What are some of the ways in which natural environments affect social organisation?

2. How does technology affect social organisation?

3. How do societies differ according to their means of subsistence?

4. What contributions can social anthropology make to the understanding of issues in ecology on a global scale?

Seminar discussion

1. Nearly all the world's hunting-and-gathering societies have now made the transition to agriculture or pastoralism. Why do you think this is?

2. Compare the means of subsistence of some of the societies you know about. To what extent are specific means of subsistence suited to particular environments?

Practical assignment

Imagine you are an advocate for the rights of indigenous peoples to pursue traditional means of subsistence. On the basis of your knowledge of relations between environment and subsistence, make a list of the arguments you would use to support your case.

Study, revision and exam tips

1 Many ethnographies begin with a description of the natural environment. When you read an ethnography, note how the environment affects the society.

2 Where relevant, look for historical connections. Archaeology and history can be relevant when cause and effect are involved. Also look for more than one variable. Neither the environment alone nor technology alone can account for every aspect of culture or society.

3 Some ecological anthropologists emphasise the influence of the environment and technology on society (e.g. Harris). Others emphasise indigenous understandings of the environment (e.g. Bird-David or Descola). Try to gauge the opinion of writers you read on this issue.

4 Economics: Interpreting Production and Distribution

One-minute overview

Economics refers to the material affairs of society. It includes production, internal distribution, and exchange with other societies. Ethnographic cases highlight cultural aspects of economic systems and shed light on the understanding of economics in the abstract. Anthropological studies have led to diverse theories of economic institutions. In this chapter you will cover:

■ how to live without a surplus
■ ways to accumulate and distribute
■ spheres of exchange in 'simple' societies
■ what is money?
■ three theories in economic anthropology

How to live without a surplus

Economics means literally 'household management'. Metaphorically, it refers to the material affairs of the society as a whole (as a giant 'household').

At one level, economics is closely related to ecology, which also has to do with material relations. Ecology relates society to the environment, whereas economics (more narrowly conceived) is what defines the material relations among people. Those in Western or East Asian 'advanced' economies may think of their societies as 'affluent' because they produce goods in surplus of their requirements. However, a case can be made for quite a different definition of 'affluence'.

The original affluent society?

Anthropologists used to think that hunter-gatherers spent all their time trying to get enough to eat, and that they simply could not produce a surplus beyond the basic level of subsistence. Hunter-gatherers, this theory goes, were unable to settle down and improve their economy until someone discovered they could grow food instead of gathering it.

That discovery sparked off the Neolithic Revolution ('new stone age' revolution). As a result, most of humanity came to plant, settle down, and develop more complex forms of social organisation. These complex forms, it was believed, enabled people to specialise in different occupations and to have more free time.

While much of this view is correct, two aspects are incorrect. Since a pioneering comparative study by American anthropologist Marshall Sahlins, we now know that:

1.   Hunter-gatherers actually spend less time in subsistence activities than most cultivators. They accumulate free time in preference to wealth.

2.   In many cases hunter-gatherers are capable of building a surplus, but they choose not to. They can get as much as they need from their environments.

The data Sahlins used were compiled by a number of hunter-gatherer specialists in the 1950s and 1960s. He published his findings in a chapter entitled 'The original affluent society', in his important book *Stone Age Economics* (1972). Since then many new studies have confirmed Sahlins' findings, and the current view is that living hunter-gatherers remain hunter-gatherers because they see their environments as 'giving' rather than requiring 'exploitation' (see chapter 3).

Question
Why should anyone adopt cultivation if life was so good as a hunter-gatherer?

Answer
Cultivation may not give people free time, but it does give them more food. The surplus can be traded or redistributed, and thereby allow some people to do work other than produce food. This is why there is a division of labour (food production, factory production, service industries, office work, etc.) in 'advanced' societies.

Furthermore (and going against Sahlins), many hunting-and-gathering peoples today do want to make the transition to intensive food production and accumulate wealth. Because of drought and pressure from neighbouring agricultural and pastoral peoples, hunter-gatherers such as Bushmen of the Kalahari can no longer sustain their 'original affluent' existence.

Yet there remains much truth in Sahlins' characterisation. Those hunter-gatherers who choose to maximise time over wealth, and who live in an environment which enables them to do this, can take what they need, then spend the rest of their time in social, ritual and leisurely pursuits. In some areas of Central Africa and in India, there are still hunter-gatherers who live this kind of existence for all or part of the annual cycle.

Ways to accumulate and distribute

The three forms of 'reciprocity'

Another contribution made in *Stone Age Economics* was the distinction between three types of reciprocity (figure 13).

Figure 13.
Balanced,
generalised
and negative
reciprocity ◀

1. Balanced reciprocity is what we usually think of by the term 'reciprocity'. Two parties each gain equally in the transaction, by buying and selling or through reciprocal gift-giving. 'A' gives something to 'B', and 'B' gives something in return, either immediately, or with a delay. Ju/'hoan (!Kung) Bushmen, for example, have a system of giving one to the other and then delayed return gifts. The delay emphasises the ongoing nature of the relationship defined by their gifts.

2. Generalised reciprocity is giving without the expectation of a return gift. An example would be parents giving to their children, or better-off people giving to poorer people, either directly or through charities.

3. Negative reciprocity is seeking to get more than one pays for, or for that matter, something for nothing. Sahlins includes barter, gambling and stealing in this category.

'The gift' and the Kwakiutl potlatch

Many point to Marcel Mauss's 'Essai sur le don' ('Essay on the gift') as the beginning of economic anthropology. The French original was published as a journal article in 1925, with two quite different English translations published in book form as *The Gift* in 1954 and 1990.

Mauss argues that exchange in 'archaic' societies is by gift, and that such societies require three obligations: to give, to receive, and to reciprocate. Furthermore, the gift 'is never free'. In other words, true generalised reciprocity does not exist. In Mauss's eyes, when one person gives to another, the recipient owes something to the donor. This may be material, or it may be something else: eg deference to the superiority of the donor or giver. Among key examples in Mauss's classic were the Trobriand kula (to be discussed shortly) and the Kwakiutl potlatch.

The Kwakiutl were traditionally a fishing, gathering and hunting people who live on Vancouver Island in British Columbia. In common with other peoples of that region, they have gift-giving ceremonies known as 'potlatches' which redistribute goods in various ways. Such redistribution enables the Kwakiutl to equalise their wealth. It also enables individual Kwakiutl to gain prestige over others by giving things away, because prestige is conferred on those who give rather than receive.

In Kwakiutl territory there is an abundance of resources. However, resources are variable. When salmon fishing is good in one area, it may be poor in another. Such variations can be seasonal, but they can also be more long-term. Traditionally, each area was owned by a kin group, with the chief of that designated custodian of the group resources. When one kin group had more food than neighbouring ones, they would hold a potlatch. The chief would collect food and other goods from kin-group members, then distribute these to a neighbouring group. The general principle is illustrated in figure 14.

Figure 14. Accumulation and redistribution
▶

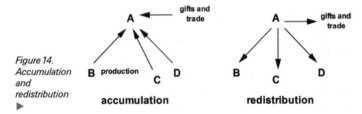

If the recipients did better the following year, they could then hold a potlatch in order to redistribute their material gains and catch up in the prestige ratings. And so it went in a never-ending cycle, until by the end of the 19th century some groups decided it would be more prestigious to destroy wealth than to give it away. Some chiefs collected and then destroyed hundreds of blankets.

In the 1920s the British Columbia government tried to put a stop to potlatching. However, the custom survived and still exists, albeit in less dramatic proportions. Today, potlatches are as likely to be held as wedding give-away ceremonies as anything else, and the goods given away include money and food.

Spheres of exchange in 'simple' societies

A sphere of exchange is simply a category of items which can be exchanged for each other, especially in societies which lack any form of money. The concept is easily understood through example. The famous case of the Trobriand will illustrate the point.

Trobriand spheres of exchange and the kula ring

The Trobriand Islanders and neighbouring seafaring peoples operate in terms of at least three major spheres: kula, wasi and gimwali. Kula, first described in Malinowski's *Argonauts of the Western Pacific* (see chapter 2), is by far the most prestigious of the spheres. It is practised especially by chiefs and other powerful men, who gain status every time they make an exchange.

Figure 15. Trobriand Islanders (© Peter Skalnik, 1988) ◄

1. Kula is the exchange of valuable armshells for equally-valuable necklaces. Trobrianders and neighbouring islanders exchange these valuables in a never-ending circle called the 'kula ring'. Necklaces pass in a clockwise direction, and armshells pass in an anti-

clockwise direction (see figure 16). The history of each item is known, and exchange partners tell the stories of their valuables when they exchange them. In formal terms, the kula comprises ceremonial exchange of non-utilitarian goods.

Figure 16. The kula ring ▼

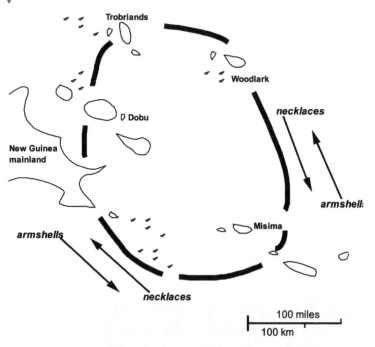

2. Wasi is the exchange of fish from lagoon villages for yams from inland villages. Like kula, it is based on standing partnerships and obligations to give and receive. In formal terms, it comprises the ceremonial exchange of utilitarian goods.

3. Gimwali is barter carried out between villagers at the time of kula. It comprises the non-ceremonial exchange of utilitarian goods except fish and yams.

Trobrianders may only exchange items in the kula sphere (armshells and necklaces) for other items in that sphere (necklaces and armshells). They cannot exchange these for yams or fish or anything else.

What is money?

Money is a commodity whose value lies not in what it is but what it can buy. It is distinguished from other commodities by the fact that it is made up of units of exchange rather than goods to be used.

Raffia cloth: commodity or money?

Another African example offers a famous case for the definition of money. Before the arrival of Belgian francs in the southern Congo, one local group, the Lele, exchanged cloths made of raffia (a palm tree) just as Belgians exchanged francs and centimes. Yet their neighbours, who wore raffia cloth as clothing, had no notion of it being anything other than that.

More specifically, to the Lele raffia cloths served some four purposes:

1. They were used as clothing. Lele men wove them, and Lele women wore them.

2. They were used in formal gift-giving or 'status payments' between kin. A young man would give 20 to his father upon his (the young man's) initiation into adulthood; he would give 20 to his wife for each child she bore him, and so on.

3. They were used as money, that is, to set the value of other goods, between non-kin. Lele purchased things like drums and drinking cups with it.

4. Lele also exchanged them for use as clothing with neighbouring peoples, who provided hoes, knives, pottery, etc. in return. In this case, it was 'money' to the Lele but a commodity of barter to the other peoples.

Defining money in an age of electronics

Complex societies such as those of the West and the Far East are dominated by money. But what is money? As the

Lele case shows, what is defined as 'money' in one society may not be seen as (all-purpose) money in another.

Put simply, money is a commodity of universal value. That is, it has a universally-agreed value within a particular society or community. The abstract nature of money was highlighted in much of the European Union in the late 1990s, in the run-up to the introduction of the euro. What ordinary people carried in their pockets were still francs, marks, guilders, pesetas, lira, and so on. Yet to economists, the 'real' unit of money was already the euro, even though there were not yet any euro coins or banknotes.

Consider also the fact that what lies in your bank account is not a pile of pounds and pence. It is an electronic record of electronically-defined units, passed from similar bank accounts held by your student grants authority or your parents to yours. If you have an overdraft, this is also an electronic record. While it may have been meaningful at one time to think of all this electronics as a cultural representation of gold or of pounds, shillings and pence, it is probably more meaningful today to think of the coins in your pocket as a representation of those electronic units which are exchanged between governments.

Three theories in economic anthropology

The theories

1. In the early days of economic anthropology there was a hidden assumption that economic systems worked pretty much the same in all cultures and societies. Those who maintained this position became known as **formalists**.

2. In the 1950s and 1960s that view was challenged by anthropologists who felt that culture affected economic attitudes, and therefore also the workings of economic systems. This position was that of the **substantivists**.

3. The 1970s saw the rise of **Marxist anthropology**, a more complex position which simultaneously borrowed from and criticised the other two positions.

Those fierce debates have died down now, but all three positions are implicit in current writings. It is important for students to have a good knowledge of them.

Formalism: economics a law unto itself

A classic formalist approach was that of American anthropologist Melville Herskovits, especially in his book *Economic Anthropology* (1952). Other formalists include Herskovits' students Edward E. LeClair Jr and Harold K. Schneider, whose 1968 edited volume, also called *Economic Anthropology*, presents better than any other the differences between the formalist and substantivist positions.

While agreeing that cultures do have differences in economic behaviour, the formalists nevertheless emphasise the similarities. They point to the fact that people everywhere 'economise'.

Basic viewpoints within the formalist position

1. Economics is a science, and economic anthropology is closely related to it.

2. Much the same laws of economics are applicable in all societies, regardless of culture.

3. The most important such law is that people behave as economically 'rational', choosing what is best for them and rejecting what is not.

4. For example, people will choose to work shorter hours, rather than longer hours, if shorter hours yield the same economic return.

5. Thus it is possible to compare different societies on questions of work effort and efficiency.

Figure 17. Market traders in Bangkok, Thailand (© Alan Barnard, 1988) ▲

Substantivism: economics embedded in culture

The substantivist position owes its origin to the writings of Hungarian-born economic historian Karl Polanyi. In *Trade and Markets in the Early Empires* (1957), he distinguished the 'substantive meaning' of the term economic (referring to the relation between making a living and one's natural and social environments) from its 'formal meaning' (referring to the logical relation between means and ends). Making use of anthropological data, he put the case for greater emphasis on the substantive aspects of economies.

Following Polanyi, a number of anthropologists came to recognise their own positions as 'substantivist'. Major figures include George Dalton, Paul Bohannan, and Marshall Sahlins. *Tribal and Peasant Economies* (1967), a collection of ethnographic papers edited by Dalton, was influential in demonstrating the case for substantivism.

Basic viewpoints within the substantivist position

1. Economics is embedded in culture. Therefore there can be no general laws of economics.

2. This is shown by the existence of different spheres of exchange, which operate differently among peoples.

3. It is also shown by different attitudes towards work,
    different values placed on the same goods in different
    societies, and different ways of thinking about exchange.
    Contrary to the formalist position, there is no agreed
    notion of 'economic rationality' which holds for all
    cultures.

4. And it is shown particularly well by the contrast between
    market economies (which may work as formalists predict
    they should) and non-market economies (to which the
    'laws of economics' don't apply).

*Figure 18.
Market
traders in
Osaka,
Japan (©
Alan
Barnard,
2002)*▼

Marxism: economics in ideology and evolution

Marxism is the product of the thinking of Karl Marx (1818-
1883). Marx's influence in economic anthropology,
however, only emerged long after his death. In the 1960s
and 1970s, French anthropologists Maurice Godelier and
Claude Meillassoux developed ways to use Marx's insights
into capitalist economic systems in the study of what they
called 'pre-capitalist' societies.

By the early 1980s, Marxism became a dominant position among economic anthropologists in the UK, as well as Scandinavia, Canada and South Africa. Useful texts include *Marxist Analyses and Social Anthropology* (edited by Maurice Bloch, 1975) and *The Anthropology of Pre-Capitalist Societies* (edited by Joel S. Kahn and Josep R. Llobera, 1981).

The idea of the mode of production (e.g. foraging, feudal, capitalist) is fundamental to Marxist anthropology. The mode consists of the 'means of production' (e.g. hunting, fishing, horticulture) plus the 'relations of production' (how people organise these activities).

Marxist anthropologists also emphasise the interaction between different modes of production. They call this interaction the articulation of modes of production. 'Pre-capitalist' economies throughout the world have long been in contact with capitalist economies which impinge upon them. This was true throughout colonial times, and is also true in the relation between traditional communities and the modern nation states of Africa, Asia, Oceania and Latin America.

Basic viewpoints within the Marxist position

1. Economics is fundamental to human social life (this is also a formalist position).

2. Economic systems can best be understood in terms of modes of production.

3. Modes of production imply social relations, and these are often relations of power (through social class, gender, etc.).

4. Modes of production each entail their respective social forms and cultural constraints (this is also a substantivist position).

5. Each mode of production contains a contradiction which can lead to it breaking down.

6. This breaking down may yield a transformation of society and the adoption of a new, more evolutionarily 'advanced' one (but not necessarily a better one for those involved in it).

7. Modes of production are often 'in articulation' and should be studied as such.

Tutorial

Progress questions

1 What is 'affluence'? Why does Sahlins regard hunter-gatherers as more 'affluent' than their agricultural neighbours?

2 What is a mode of production? What is a sphere of exchange? How are these concepts useful in analysing economic systems?

3 Describe the differences between the three theoretical positions mentioned in this chapter.

Seminar discussion

1 Put yourself in the position of a hunter-gatherer in a desert environment. Consider how you would utilise its resources. Evaluate the trade-offs between accumulation of goods and free time.

2 Consider 'the gift' in your own society. What social values are implicit in gift giving? What is the true 'value' of 'the gift': its monetary value or its social value?

3 Think about how theory in economic anthropology has changed through time. Consider why these changes might have occurred. What changes within anthropology are relevant (new ethnographic data, for example)? What changes in the world beyond anthropology are relevant (the Cold War, or student revolt in the 1960s)?

Practical assignment

Find a few willing informants among students of economics, business studies or accountancy. Interview them about their perceptions of economics as they understand it. Analyse what they say in light of your own understanding of economic systems (Kwakiutl, Lele, etc.). Try to discover in this way the cultural assumptions about economics in your own society.

Study, revision and exam tips

1. When you read ethnographic cases, think about their theoretical implications. For example, a study of spheres of exchange might imply a substantivist approach. A study of work effort might imply a formalist one.

2. In essays and exams, discuss work which you disagree with, as well as work you agree with. Do not assume your reader will agree with you: always argue a good case.

3. Where appropriate, use diagrams such as those in figures 13 and 14 to illustrate points in your essays and exams. These can be ones from lectures or books or your own ones. When you copy other people's diagrams exactly, you should cite the source.

5

Politics and Law: Discerning Power and Social Control

One-minute overview

Politics includes relations of power and authority, strategies of decision-making, and the structures for social control (such as bands, tribes, chiefdoms and states). Political anthropology focuses on these things and also on issues like ethnicity and nationalism. The anthropological study of law is related to political anthropology. Its emphasis is on the comparative study of law, especially in small-scale societies. In this chapter you will cover:

■ approaches to politics
■ studying levels of political organisation
■ seeking the origin of the state
■ explaining social stratification
■ appreciating ethnicity and nationalism
■ is 'law' universal?

Approaches to politics

In anthropology there are a number of possible ways to approach the study of political systems. It is wise to be aware of these, as what you read may be biased towards one approach over another. Also, your lecturer or tutor may favour one method over another.

The basic approaches are:

1. typological
2. functionalist
3. dynamic

4. Marxist
5. terminological.

The typological and terminological approaches

- *The typological approach* – This involves the classification of societies into different types. In some respects this is the simplest approach, and is illustrated below under the heading 'Studying levels of political organisation'. The types illustrated there are based on the evolutionary development of political structures from simple to complex. A leading proponent of that idea has been American anthropologist Elman Service, for example in his book *Profiles in Ethnology* (1978).

- *The terminological approach* – This emphasises the definition of concepts over the definition of types. Jamaican anthropologist M.G. Smith, for example, sought to explain political action and political power, authority and administration, etc., in his 1960 book on Nigerian state politics, *Government in Zazau*. Smith was interested in concepts which would be applicable to all political systems. In more recent times, the emphasis has moved more towards concepts based on indigenous understandings and therefore applicable in specific instances.

The functionalist and structuralist approaches

These are based on the broad theoretical perspectives which go by these labels (see chapter 10).

- *Functionalists* – These include mainly British and South African anthropologists, like A.R. Radcliffe-Brown, Meyer Fortes and Isaac Schapera, writing mainly from the 1920s to the 1970s. Their approach emphasises the ways in which politics and government relate to other aspects of social structure, such as economics, kinship and religion.

- *Structuralists* – These include British, French and other anthropologists, though this approach has not been as prominent in the study of politics as it has in areas such as kinship and religion. Sir Edmund Leach in *Political Systems of Highland Burma* (1954) is an early example. Leach talks of social processes which create oscillation between two types of social organisation among the Kachin of Burma: gumsa (hierarchical) and gumlao (egalitarian). His study is 'structuralist' in that he describes social relations in a context of Kachin structures of belief, including beliefs about the part believed to be played by ancestral spirits in the political order.

- *The dynamic and Marxist approaches* – In *Order and Rebellion in Tribal Africa* (1963), South African Max Gluckman, argued that a more **dynamic** approach is needed. He suggested that rebellion is a permanent process and makes sense in political systems in which instability is regarded as normal. His approach was an attack on the oversimplification of functionalists who saw politics in traditional societies as simple and static. Many follow his lead today. **Marxists**, especially in the 1970s and 1980s, went further. As we saw in the last chapter, they looked to what they called the 'articulation of modes of production'. In Marxist jargon, this refers to the interaction between economies which come into contact, as when hunter-gatherers come into contact with herders, or subsistence farmers with colonial or state capitalist bureaucracies.

Figure 19. Can instability be regarded as normal? The divided city of Mostar, Bosnia-Herzegovena (© Kimberley Coles, 1997) ▼

Question – If professional anthropologists cannot agree, how can a first-year student decide which approach is best?

Answer – There are two possible answers. On the one hand, a student should decide which approach is best for the specific task at hand. For example, if you are interested in relations between different economies, then a Marxist approach might be best, even if it isn't best for discussion of other issues.

The other possible answer is that a first-year student, having assessed the evidence, is in a very good position to make a sound judgement. One doesn't need to be a politician in order to vote for one. Likewise, one doesn't need to be an anthropological theorist in order to decide which theory makes sense.

Studying levels of political organisation

A classic division of societies is according to whether the primary political unit is the band, tribe, chiefdom or state.

Band societies

Characteristics of band societies typically include:

1. economy based on hunting and gathering (or occasionally fishing or horticulture)

2. social structure based on ties of kinship

3. relative equality between the sexes

4. egalitarian way of life: no-one has superiority over anyone else

5. de-emphasis on leadership, which in any case tends to be unspecialised and temporary (such as for a hunting expedition)

6. decisions taken by consensus

A typical example is the G/wi Bushmen, described by George Silberbauer in *Hunter and Habitat in the Central Kalahari Desert* (1981). G/wi have traditionally lived in bands averaging some 50 or 60 people. Bands would migrate within their respective territories and disperse seasonally. When there are disputes, band members discuss the issues and co-operate in finding a solution. Even those who disagree tend to abide by such decisions, without formal judgements or coercion.

Like many band societies, the way of life of the G/wi is under serious threat today. They were thrown out of their traditional lands in 2002, and their right to those lands has since then been the subject of ongoing court battles in the Republic of Botswana.

Tribal societies

Characteristics may include:

1. economy based on livestock or horticulture

2. social structure based on clans or lineages

3. age and gender are often important factors

4. sometimes 'acephalous' (literally 'headless', without leaders)

5. sometimes with leaders, usually ones who gain influence through favours for others and the accumulation of wealth (such as the 'big men' in Papua New Guinea)

A well-known example is the Nuer of Sudan. Traditional Nuer society is an acephalous rather than a 'big man' one. Political authority is in the hands of lineages and local groups which are very loosely based on kinship: there is some argument among anthropologists as to how loosely Nuer disputes involve groups of various sizes, and these pay damages in the event of wrongs committed by their members. If there is no agreement, the two sides call in a 'leopard-skin chief' (as Evans-Pritchard called him).

Actually, he is not a chief at all but an impartial judge and ritual priest.

Chiefly societies

Typically these include:

1. economy based on livestock, horticulture or intensive agriculture

2. government by hereditary chiefs

3. chiefs having power and authority, and often inherited wealth

4. chiefs acting as judges in disputes, distributing land, redistributing produce, etc.

5. sometimes chiefs having supernatural power by virtue of their positions (such as in Polynesia, where chiefs are believed to possess a supernatural power called mana)

The Trobrianders are an example. The office of chief is held by males but is hereditary in the female line (a man inherits from his mother's brother). Yet as in other Melanesian societies, chiefs differ in their abilities to exercise power. One way they can exercise power is by controlling the distribution of yams. The best way to do this is to be married to several women at the same time: wives collect yams from their relatives. Chiefs also perform magical spells to give them control over both the yams and the people of their respective villages.

State societies

Among the characteristics of state societies are:

1. economy based on intensive agriculture and often a developed market system

2. relatively high population density

3. sometimes extensive trade networks, both internal and external

4. often powerful military organisation to keep control over the population and/or to subjugate dependent populations

5. social stratification on class or caste principles

6. hereditary or elected leaders with power over others

7. sometimes leaders having sacred duties or supernatural power (such as in some African kingdoms)

One example is the Swazi kingdom in Southern Africa. They represent one of Africa's many pre-colonial kingdoms which have continued to the present day, though one of the few that has the status of a nation-state (Swaziland). Others, such as the neighbouring Zulu kingdom in South Africa, are incorporated into modern republics. Swaziland is today a constitutional monarchy, but the king and his mother, as well as district and local chiefs, maintain traditional authority over many aspects of Swazi life.

Seeking the origin of the state

There are different theories of how states came into being. Here are four important ones.

1. Hydraulic theory

This was proposed by Karl Wittfogel in *Oriental Despotism: A Comparative Study of Total Power*, 1957. This argues that early states developed because of the invention and spread of systems of irrigation. These involved the necessity to control the labour of large numbers of people.

2. Coercive theory

This was proposed by Robert Carneiro in an article in *Science* magazine (1970). It asserts that states first emerged because of warfare in places with limited agricultural land. Carneiro used the example of the Inca of Peru, but suggested that similar mechanisms operated elsewhere, notably in the Nile and Indus valleys and in ancient Mesopotamia. Pressures kept increasing as populations experienced warfare between villages. Those who won subjugated those who lost and built up their power structures.

3. Class theory

This dates from the work of Karl Marx and Friedrich Engels, especially Engels' book *The Origin of the Family, Private Property and the State* (1884). Engels, and his followers in more recent times, argued that states arose as a result of antagonisms between social classes. The ruling classes kept others in line by perpetuating the 'myth' that the state is necessary for the preservation of order.

4. Social contract theory

Figure 20. In many modern societies the state is pervasive: here Palestinian women pass through an Israeli checkpoint (© Tobias Kelly, 2001)
▼

This is even earlier, dating from the work of Thomas Hobbes, John Locke, Jean-Jacques Rousseau in the 17th and 18th centuries. The idea is that at some point in time, primitive people decided to give up liberty in order to have a social order, and this order became the state. Anthropology distinguishes sharply between the state and society, and therefore this theory holds little for anthropologists who specialise in small-scale, stateless societies. Yet it remains implicit in political and legal thinking.

The current consensus

The consensus today is that many factors, in several different places, led to the creation of states. Ethnographic data on stateless as well as on state societies are useful to those in other disciplines, from archaeology to law, who are concerned with this topic.

Explaining social stratification

The detailed explanation of social stratification is usually the preserve of sociology, but it is useful for anthropology students too to know a few essential concepts.

Class societies

Class societies are those which are stratified by the unequal access to political power or economic goods. There can be cultural aspects to class as well, which may be only indirectly related to politics and economics. For example in England, working class, middle class and upper class people differ in what they eat and drink, what sports they enjoy, how they decorate their houses, and how they speak. In many societies, class membership is more fluid than in England. The United States, where class is defined more by economics than by culture, is an obvious example.

Caste societies

Caste societies are those such as India, where stratification is more rigid than by class. These have long occupied the attention of anthropologists, the most famous being the French author Louis Dumont in books such as *Homo Hierarchicus* (1967).

India

In India the castes have not only an economic but also a ritual and religious significance. People in higher castes are believed to be superior by virtue of their greater 'purity'. People in lower castes are said to be 'polluting'. Purity and pollution derive from caste membership; at the same time the occupations traditionally practised by each caste specifically confirms this ritual status. Leatherworking is a low status occupation, and leather itself is believed to be polluting. Cooking is a high status occupation, and certain foods, such as rice, are believed to be ritually pure. Indians tend to marry within their caste or to members of a similar caste (jati).

There are actually two quite different forms of caste in India:

1. The **jatis** are the real social groups and have both an occupational basis and a local basis. Relative status varies in different parts of India, and particular jatis have been known to change their status by engaging collectively in 'purer', less 'polluting' activities.

2. The **varnas**, on the other hand, are large, idealised caste divisions. There are four of these, each associated with a traditional occupational category (figure 21). Below members of the varnas are the Harijan or members of 'scheduled castes' (formerly called 'untouchables'), who traditionally held the lowest-status and least-pleasant occupations.

Figure 21. The four varnas and their traditional occupations
▼

varna	traditional occupation
Brahman	priest
Kshatriya	nobleman and warrior
Vaishya	commoner and farmer
Shudra	serf or servant

Other forms of stratification

Not all societies are stratified. Most band societies and some tribal societies are essentially egalitarian, and the one way to explain stratification is as a development away from such structures. Such developments may occur where whole groups take control (as in Leach's study of Burma, perhaps leading to caste structures) or where individuals achieve power through control over resources (perhaps leading to class structures). The latter case is characteristic of the situation with 'big men' in Papua New Guinea (see Maurice Godelier's *The Making of Great Men*, 1986).

Appreciating ethnicity and nationalism

Ethnicity has long been a topic of interest in anthropology, and the study of nationalism is growing in importance. The topics are closely related.

The major figure in the study of ethnicity is Norwegian anthropologist Fredrik Barth, who did fieldwork in many parts of Asia and the Pacific. In *Political Leadership among Swat Pathans* (1959), he showed that the position of leaders is dependent on maintaining the allegiance of the people through transactions and oscillation between conflict and coalition. He developed these ideas further in the introduction to his edited book *Ethnic Groups and Boundaries* (1969), which inspired many to look at ethnicity not as a given, but as something people define for themselves and negotiate like political power. Since then many have used his ideas in studying nationalism in many contexts. Different points of emphasis have arisen. For example in the study of the post-Communist Eastern Europe, some have emphasised continuity with the old political structures, whereas others emphasise newfound national identities and connections with pre-Communist ways of life.

Nationalism does not always imply a nation state, and is often equated with ethnic identity. Scottish nationalism, for example, has an element of Scottish ethnic identity (although not all Scottish nationalists are ethnic Scots). Likewise, Palestinian nationalism is related to Palestinian ethnicity as well as to the desire for an independent state (see figures 20 and 22).

Figure 22. A Palestinian shopkeeper with friends; on the wall behind them are Palestinian nationalist slogans (© Tobias Kelly, 2001)

Three perspectives

Over the years, three main perspectives of ethnicity and nationalism have emerged:

1. *Primordialist perspectives* – view ethnicity and nationalism as rooted in real characteristics of peoples and nations, created by factors like biology, geography and language. Nationalists often take this view.

2. *Instrumentalist perspectives* – see ethnicity and nationalism as creations of a political elite to serve their own purposes. Marxists (among others) often take this view.

3. *Constructivist perspectives* – see ethnic and national identities as products of particular situations. Individuals construct identities which are meaningful to them and which they can manipulate. Barth's approach fits in here.

Is 'law' universal?

Many 19th-century anthropologists were lawyers. Some, such as Sir Henry Maine, author of *Ancient Law* (1861), had a specific interest in the origin and development of law.

Maine believed that the evolution from kinship-based to contract-based forms of organisation was characteristic of the advance of human society.

In the 20th century, several anthropologists examined the legal systems of 'tribal' societies and found them sophisticated, complex, and sometimes (especially in Africa) having great similarities to the systems of modern national states. Yet this still leaves open the question of the universality of law.

Three possible universals

Malinowski in *Crime and Custom in Savage Society* (1926) saw little or no difference between law and custom. In this perspective, law would certainly be a cultural universal.

American anthropologist E. Adamson Hoebel, who trained originally as a lawyer, objected to such a broad definition of law but nevertheless agreed that it is a universal. In *The Law of Primitive Man* (1954) he emphasised coercion as the defining principle. More specifically, law entails three universal principles:

(a) the legitimate use of force to ensure correct behaviour and punish wrongdoing

(b) the allocation of power to individuals (such as the police in modern societies) to use coercion

(c) the respect for tradition as against whim: enforcement must be based on the existence of known rules, whether customs or statutes.

These principles seem to apply almost everywhere, though the second might be problematic among some hunter-gatherers. But do they really define what we mean by 'law' in all societies?

Later writers, such as Sally Falk Moore (in *Law as Process*, 1978) have emphasised the dynamic nature of legal systems:

the pressures which provide the need for law also provide the need for changes in the law.

African customary law

One of the most important legal anthropologists was Max Gluckman (1911–1975), mentioned above. Gluckman was a South African who emigrated to Britain and taught for many years at the University of Manchester. Important in Gluckman's work was the idea that anthropology should focus on change, social processes, rebellion and conflict, rather than stability. His books include titles like *Custom and Conflict in Africa* (1955) and *Order and Rebellion in Tribal Africa* (1963). If reading such works, note the distinction between rebellion (which is about displacing people who are in power) and revolution (which is about changing the system in which power operates). Gluckman's main concern was with the former.

In recent studies, some have focused on relations between different legal systems within the same country.

- *Example* – Consider the law of Botswana, which has as one of its bases 'customary law', that is, the traditional legal system of the Tswana people (and the authority of tribal chiefs and democratic outdoor meetings). Another is 'common law' (English in origin). Yet while Botswana has

▲
Figure 23. An extended family in eastern Botswana (© Alan Barnard, 1982)
▶

a criminal law system based on the English one, it has a civil law system similar to the Scots one, which in turn is related to Roman-Dutch Law. Lawyer-anthropologist Anne Griffiths has written on the difficulties in women's access to legal process in this complex situation in her book *In the Shadow of Marriage* (1997).

A question of current concern, both theoretical and practical, is the universality of human rights. As usually defined, 'human rights' are rights which individuals have, irrespective of the society they live in. Yet it has been argued that in some African societies the concept of the individual is only meaningful in terms of the community to which he or she belongs. Does the notion of 'human rights' depend on a Western emphasis on the individual over the community? This is a question which will undoubtedly engage anthropologists in the future.

Tutorial

Progress questions

1. What are some of the main approaches to the study of politics in anthropology?

2. What are the classic types of political organisation as defined by anthropologists? What are their characteristics?

3. Can you name four theories of the origin of the state? Three perspectives on ethnicity and nationalism? Three possible universal principles in law?

Seminar discussion

1. Discuss the proposition that 'power corrupts', using examples from your anthropological reading.

2. Does the notion of 'human rights' depend on a Western emphasis on the individual over the community?

Practical assignment

Try a role-playing exercise in decision-making. First, make the decision by consensus as in a band society. Then act out a dispute involving members of two different kin groups, as in a tribal society. Then try the same for a chiefly society and a society where the state operates through powerful individuals, either elected or otherwise.

Study, revision and exam tips

1. List theories, perspectives and explanations of aspects of politics. Think how to use these in debating an issue or writing an exam answer.

2. Pay attention not just to concepts which are familiar, but also to those which are familiar (such as politics or law).

3. Look at both small and big issues, and be aware of the difference. For example, you might be asked in an essay or exam to explain the workings of law in a specific traditional African society (a relatively small question), or you might be asked to explain whether 'law' is a cultural universal (a bigger question).

6

Belief, Ritual and Symbolism

Belief, ritual and symbolism are complex aspects of culture. Anthropologists try to interpret them without the prejudice of their own belief systems. They have devised concepts drawn from the study of many societies and methods based on both observation and intuition. Crucial distinctions, such as sacred and profane, or witchcraft and sorcery, make the task easier. By seeking the structure of mythology and symbolism, some anthropologists are able to find meaning in what at first appears a meaningless jumble. In this chapter you will cover:

■ different views of the world
■ the sacred and the profane
■ understanding belief systems
■ explaining witchcraft and sorcery
■ encountering ritual
■ interpreting mythology and symbolism

Different views of the world

Topics like ecological anthropology and the anthropology of economics and politics are rather 'hard' areas of the discipline. Their study requires a style of documentation and analysis which can be quite different from the study of belief, ritual and symbolism.

The anthropological study of religion, or more precisely the study of belief, ritual and symbolism, is 'soft' in the sense of being more interpretive. Anthropologists interested in religion are more likely to try to think like their informants and understand their vision of the world.

Question – How do anthropologists reconcile their own beliefs about the world with writing about the beliefs of others?

Answer – There is a convention in anthropology that writers treat beliefs as true for the believers, and do not comment on whether they are true in the sense of representing an external reality.

Question – Does this mean they accept all religions as true?

Answer – Not exactly. It simply means that they separate theological truth from what might be called anthropological truth (what people in society say and do) and comment only on the latter.

Question – Does this mean that all anthropologists are atheists?

Answer – Not at all. Anthropologists include practising Buddhists, Hindus, Christians, Jews, Muslims and other groups, and many have specialised in the study of religions other than their own.

The sacred and the profane

The most fundamental distinction between studies of belief, ritual and symbolism, on the one hand, and virtually all the rest of anthropological studies on the other, is the notion of the 'sacred'. In *The Elementary Forms of the Religious Life* (1912), French sociologist Emile Durkheim made an important distinction between the 'sacred' and the 'profane'. The distinction has been reiterated by anthropologists and religious studies scholars ever since, most famously by Romanian writer Mircea Eliade in *The Sacred and the Profane* (1957).

Sacred
1. set apart from the normal world
2. may entail 'forbidden' knowledge or practices (taboos)

3. includes ritual practices
4. often associated with magical forces, spirits or deities
5. related to what we normally think of as religion, as well as magical practices.

Profane

1. belonging to the normal world
2. entails everyday knowledge
3. includes utilitarian practices
4. associated with ordinary, especially material things
5. related to what we think of as non-religious activities or aspects of culture.

Figure 24. Sacred temple procession, Bhutan (© Richard Whitecross, 2004)
◀

Figure 25. Secular (mundane) folk dance being performed within sacred religious rites in Bhutan (© Richard Whitecross, 2004)
◀

It is worth considering the possibility that these two categories are not enough. Some anthropologists working with Australian Aborigines have suggested that it makes sense to think in terms of a third category: the 'mundane'. This would include things that are too ordinary even to be thought of as 'non-sacred' (profane).

Understanding belief systems

Anthropologists used to spend a great deal of effort classifying systems of belief. This was partly because early anthropologists were interested in the evolution of religion. Complex classification schemes are no longer common, but it remains important to know a few key concepts.

Animism and fetishism

Animism is the belief in spirits inhabiting things like mountains, rivers, rocks and trees. Early anthropologists, notably Sir Edward Burnett Tylor (1832–1917), thought that this was the oldest form of religion. Animistic beliefs are common in many parts of the world.

Early anthropologists also regarded fetishism as an ancient form of religion. 'Primitive' peoples supposedly made fetishes, objects they believed to have magical powers. We now know that although fetishes exist, they do not form the basis of anything that can be described as a belief system.

Totemism

Totemism is a complicated matter. The term is broadly taken to mean the symbolic representation of social phenomena by natural phenomena.

The word totem is from the Ojibwa language, spoken in the Great Lakes region of North America. It was introduced to English as early as 1791. In Ojibwa thought, totem is contrasted to manitoo. Ojibwa totems are spiritual entities represented by an animal species (such as catfish, crane and bear). There are several, and each symbolises a different clan. They are found in the mythology, and you cannot marry a person with the same totem as yourself. Manitoos are the guardian spirits of individuals rather than groups. They come in dreams, and you cannot kill or eat the animal species which is your manitoo.

Similar notions are found in other cultures. For example, ethnographers in Australia have reported a variety of different kinds of 'totem'. Among others, there are:

- *individual totems* – which resemble the manitoos of the Ojibwa

- *clan totems* – like those of the Ojibwa

- *sacred-site totems* – which belong to spirits of sacred sites.

In Australia, totems represent beings whose flesh cannot be eaten and whose fellow members cannot be taken as lovers or spouses. So they tend to incorporate the abstract principles of both the Ojibwa manitoos and the Ojibwa totems.

Totemic beliefs are also recorded in South America, Asia, Africa, and the Pacific. Yet for all that is written on 'totemism', many anthropologists (famously, Alexander Goldenweiser in a 1910 article, and Claude Lévi-Strauss in his 1962 book called *Totemism*) have said that there is no such thing! At its simplest level, their argument is that 'totemism' differs so much from place to place that it is not a single phenomenon, but several. More specifically, there is a great difference between 'totems' which are simply emblems for clans or other social groups, and those which also entail food prohibitions and a range of other sacred associations.

Shamanism

Most religions involve religious experts or specialists in the performance of ritual: priests, rabbis, etc. In the anthropological literature, one kind of ritual specialist that has been discussed extensively is the shaman.

A shaman (plural shamans) is a person who mediates between the human world and the spirit world, between humans and animals, or between the living and the dead. The term is essentially synonymous with 'medicine man', 'wizard', or in some usages 'magician'. It comes from the language of the Tungus people of eastern Siberia, but has been extended to cover similar ritual specialists throughout the world, especially in the Arctic, South America, and to some extent Africa. Sometimes, such a person may heal others by communicating with ancestral spirits. Such traditional healers in Zimbabwe held a special place in that country's liberation struggle.

Figure 26. Traditional healer (on the right) with her husband and assistant, Zimbabwe (© Joost Fontein, 1995) ▼

The classic statement on shamanism and related beliefs is that of Eliade in his book *Shamanism* (1954), which covers the phenomenon in several continents.

Monotheism and polytheism

Monotheistic religions are those that assert that there is one God. Judaism, Christianity, Islam, and many indigenous African religions are examples. Polytheistic religions are those that accept the existence of more than one deity. Ancient Egyptian, Greek, and Roman religions are examples.

However, the distinction between monotheism and polytheism is not always clear-cut. The Nuer and Dinka of Sudan, for example, are essentially monotheistic, but they also talk of divinities or spirits of various kinds. Evans-Pritchard's *Nuer Religion* (1956) begins with chapters on God (called kwoth), the 'spirits of above' (also called kwoth, or kuth in the plural), and the 'spirits of below' (again, kwoth or kuth). Furthermore, kwoth can mean simply 'breath' (compare Latin spiritus, also meaning both 'breath' and 'spirit').

Cargo cults

In several parts of the world, most importantly in Melanesia and the Pacific, people have believed that at the end of the world or dawn of a new age their ancestors will return with a 'cargo' of valuable goods. Such movements were especially prevalent in the aftermath of the Second World War (1939-45). Prophets have predicted these returns and encouraged people to build docks or airfields, so that the ancestors could bring valuable, especially Western goods like the latest clothing, radios, refrigerators, and motor vehicles. Peter Lawrence's *Road Belong Cargo* (1964) is a famous case study.

Among Native North Americans similar religious beliefs are found, and these are usually called nativistic movements or (more broadly) revitalisation movements.

Explaining witchcraft and sorcery

Although sometimes together called 'magic', it can be important to distinguish witchcraft from sorcery.

- *Witchcraft* – is commonly defined as a malevolent magical practice which is, at least in part, inherent in the makeup of an individual. People are born to be witches, or become witches through an evil substance within them which they have little or no control over.

- *Sorcery* – is similar in its effects, but it is learned rather than inherited.

The distinction within anthropology actually rests on a similar distinction made by the Zande (Azande) people of Sudan and the Democratic Republic of Congo and recorded by Evans-Pritchard in W*itchcraft, Oracles and Magic among the Azande* (1937).

The Zande are captivated by witchcraft. They understand many things as having two causes; one will be a physical cause, and the other will involve sorcery or, more often, witchcraft. If termites eat the supports from a grain storage bin and it falls and kills someone, one level of explanation will be that termites ate the supports. But that is not enough for the Zande. They need to explain also why it fell at that particular time on that particular person. This can only be explained by malevolence on the part of someone else: a witch will have placed that person there at that time and caused the bin to fall then.

This is an extreme case, because the Zande are so bound up in witchcraft beliefs and witchcraft accusations, but it does give a very real sense of the kind of explanation offered in African societies that accept witchcraft as a part of everyday life. Evans-Pritchard's method of explanation, and that of other anthropologists since, was to reflect this indigenous understanding and try to relate it to other aspects of (in this case Zande) culture and society. Witchcraft and sorcery are still practised, or alleged to be practised (since few admit to these activities) in many societies. Anthropologists have studied their alleged practices, for example in supermarkets in South Africa.

Encountering ritual

Sacrifice

Sacrifice is a central element of nearly all religions. Anthropologists take the term in a very wide sense. It is not essential that it involves giving up something valuable, but only that a symbolic gesture is made.

This can be a gesture recognising the presence of a spirit or ancestor. For example, Chinese mourners place rice on the graves of their deceased relatives, and in many African societies people pour a very small amount of drink onto the ground for spirits or ancestors before drinking themselves.

Extreme cases such as human sacrifice (as among the Aztecs) are very rare. More typically, we think of animal sacrifice; a goat or a cow, slaughtered for the ancestors or deities but actually eaten by the living people who perform the sacrifice. Evans-Pritchard's account of sacrifice in *Nuer Religion* (1956) is a classic.

Rites of passage

A rite of passage is a ceremony an individual goes through to mark the change from one status in life to another. Common ones include:

- *naming rites* – marking the transition from non-person to person or from person outside the community to person within the community

- *initiation rites* – marking the transition from childhood to adulthood

- *marriage rites* – marking the transition from single to married status

- *funeral rites* – marking the transition from person to ancestor, or from person within the community of the living to person beyond.

An example of a naming rite familiar to many would be a christening or baptism in Christianity. An example of an initiation rite would be confirmation in Christianity or a bar mitsvah or bat mitsvah in Judaism.

Marriage rites are found in every society. They often have a religious basis, though this is not essential for them to be considered rites of passage. Indeed even divorce proceedings in a courtroom can be considered (secular) rites of passage, reversing the 'single' to 'married' transition of the rite of marriage.

Funerals are also universal. The specific meaning will depend on the system of religious belief. In some societies more than one funeral is necessary, and sometimes even more than one burial ceremony. On Madagascar and in much of Aboriginal Australia, an individual is buried once, then his or her body dug up and buried again, to mark these phases in the transition from living to ancestral status.

The key writer on rights of passage was the French folklorist Arnold van Gennep, whose book *The Rites of Passage* (1909) paved the way for future research on this topic. Van Gennep argued that all rites of passage involve three phases:

(a) separation (such as leaving the group prior to rituals)

(b) transition (the period of most ritual activity)

(c) incorporation (where individuals are re-introduced to the group in their new status).

The transition phase is frequently called that of liminality (from the Latin limen, for 'threshold'). In this phase, there are often rituals of 'reversal', where for example men act as if they are women or old people act as if they are children.

Example – the naven ceremony

One famous example is the naven ceremony of the Iatmul of Papua New Guinea. It was described by Gregory Bateson in his book *Naven* (1936). Their rituals involve transvestism, homosexual acts, and the purposeful violation of taboos which in other contexts regulate kinship and gender relations. These activities are permissible only as ritual acts in such a liminal phase and not in everyday Iatmul life.

Example – male initiation ceremony

Another famous example is the male initiation ceremony of the Ndembu of Zambia, described by Victor Turner in *The Forest of Symbols* (1967). Turner stressed the special bonds formed among people involved in the liminal phase and called this 'communitas'. Communitas is, in a sense, the opposite of normal social structure. As among the Iatmul, Ndembu communitas involves the violation of normal rules of behaviour and at the same time a heightened sense of group solidarity. In later life, Turner sought to explain the idea of pilgrimage (a religious journey which is both physical and spiritual) in terms of communitas.

Interpreting mythology and symbolism

One viewpoint frequently used to interpret mythology is that it is a 'charter for social action'. The phrase originates with Malinowski. What he meant was that myths embody the rules for correct social behaviour. To those who believe in them, myths explain; relations between social groups and between categories of relatives; whom to marry, what one can and cannot eat and why, etc.

Another common view, and the one we shall briefly explore here, is that of a structural interpretation. The chief proponent of structural interpretations is the French anthropologist Claude Lévi-Strauss. Between 1964 and 1970 he wrote four volumes on mythology, which together are called the *Mythologiques* (an invented word; a literal English translation would be 'mythologics') and contain analyses of 813 myths from North and South America. Among other works on mythology, and one drawn on below, is his famous essay 'The story of Asdiwal', published in French in 1958 and reprinted many times (see Lévi-Strauss, *Structural Anthropology 2*, 1973).

Figure 27.
Claude Lévi-
Strauss doing
fieldwork in
Brazil, ca. 1937
▶

Mythology

The central point about mythology, from a structuralist
point of view, is that it is not random. It is comprised of
myths which make sense both internally and in relation to
other myths.

Example

The myth of Asdiwal was originally collected by Frans Boas
among the Tsimshian people of British Columbia. In the

myth, Asdiwal moves back and forth between two rivers running parallel to each other, and back and forth again between the coast and the upper reaches of each river. The myth begins with the migration of Asdiwal's mother and grandmother from a famine area, and ends with Asdiwal being turned to stone in the frozen wastes. Throughout the myth, Asdiwal's adventures lead him to hunt several animals and marry three women, one of whom bears him a son. Other characters include his father, who is (or is represented by) a bird, and rival brothers-in-law by his various marriages.

Analysing the myth

The details are not important here. What is important is the analysis of the myth. Boas only recorded it, but Lévi-Strauss uncovered its structural meaning. According to Lévi-Strauss, the myth can be understood in terms of some six 'schema': geographical, cosmological, integrative, sociological, techno-economic, and global.

For example, on the geographical level, we can talk about Asdiwal's movements from east to west and north to south. The latter correspond, more or less, to real migrations of the Tsimshian people in their quest for seasonally-available fish (and to the techno-economic level). The global level involves the integration of oppositional elements, like male and female, feast and famine, in the myth.

When all these elements are understood in relation to each other, Lévi-Strauss argues, we can uncover not just the meaning of the myth, but the deeper thought processes of the Tsimshian people, and perhaps those of humankind in general.

Symbolism

Structural anthropologists suggest that it is much the same with any aspect of symbolism. Spatial symbolism is perhaps the easiest to understand, because it is visual.

There have been many studies in anthropology of the layout of villages and of buildings, especially houses. Frequently, there is a distinction between the inside and outside of the village, which may imply a symbolic distinction between culture (inside) and nature (outside). Houses are often divided between public and private areas, male and female areas, and so on. Though these do not necessarily carry a religious meaning, they are nevertheless symbolic of social relations.

There are also examples of spatial symbolism in ritual. A traditional British wedding is one example. The bride's side is on the left, the groom's on the right. People are seated according to this convention. The bride enters on her father's left arm and leaves on her husband's right arm.

We shall look further at the symbolism of gender itself in the next chapter, but for now the important point is that symbolic order is predicated on simple oppositions like right and left. For people who engage in a ritual, live in a house, or do almost anything, these carry meaning. It is the job of anthropologists to find this meaning.

Tutorial

Progress questions

1 Explain the difference between 'sacred' and 'profane'.

2 What is totemism? Why have some anthropologists said there is no such thing?

3 What is the difference between witchcraft and sorcery?

4 What are rites of passage? Give some examples.

5 How have anthropologists tried to explain mythology and symbolism?

Seminar discussion

Are belief, ritual and symbolism intrinsically more complex and more difficult for anthropologists to come to grips with, than are studies of mundane things like economics or politics?

Practical assignments

Visit a familiar place of worship. Write an ethnographic description of what you observe, including both the surroundings and the ritual activities which go on there. Can you offer an explanation similar to those of anthropologists in alien cultures?

Study, revision and exam tips

1 In anthropology essays and exams, avoid making your own religious beliefs explicit when writing on the beliefs of others. Unlike in theology, only the latter are relevant.

2 Also avoid the use of the word believe, except in the context of religion or worldview. Use argue instead. For example, do not say 'Durkheim believes...' but rather 'Durkheim argues...' – not 'I believe Durkheim's theory', but 'I accept Durkheim's argument'.

3 Learn the terminology anthropologists have devised to explain things, such as rites of passage and shamanism, and use them in your essays and exams. When comparing similar phenomena (such as 'totemism') in different cultures, consider whether they really are the same.

4 Consider the advantages of each theoretical perspective for the analysis of specific aspects of culture or society. For example, it is sometimes said that structuralism is appropriate for the analysis of mythology.

7

Sex, Gender and the Family

One-minute overview

Sex concerns biology, and gender concerns social and cultural behaviour. Anthropologists have made studies of gender in different societies, but more importantly they have made cross-cultural comparisons and looked for evidence for and against universal features of sex and gender. The feminist critique has been especially powerful in making anthropologists think about such issues. Likewise, cross-cultural studies of the family and marriage have shown that what we often take for granted as universal is not so. In this chapter you will cover:

■ comparing gender roles and attitudes to sex
■ explaining gender: two views
■ liberating women and men: the feminist critique
■ how families and marriage differ in different societies

Comparing gender roles and attitudes to sex

In anthropology, sex refers both to sexual activity and to the biological distinction between female and male. Gender refers to social or cultural distinctions, and these differ from place to place.

Explanation of gender roles

In terms of the division of labour, men and women typically have different activities:

1. Hunting, herding and fishing are predominantly male activities, while food-gathering is a female activity.

2. Cultivation differs from society to society; sometimes it is done by males and sometimes by females.

3. In the domestic sphere, women do most of the childcare
   and the cleaning in most societies.

Making clothing can be either a female or a male activity,
and building houses is similarly divided.

Example

Among the Nharo (or: Naro) Bushmen of Botswana, men
hunt and do a little food-gathering, while women do most
food-gathering and the fetching of water and firewood. In
building houses, men do the heavy work of cutting
branches, while women do the thatching. Men make their
own clothes, and women make theirs. Mothers carry babies
on their backs, but fathers, grandparents, and brothers and
sisters all participate in child-rearing. Men and women have
separate roles in rituals, but there is gender equality and
relatively little differentiation in other activities.

*Figure 28.
Nharo women
thatching a roof
(© Alan
Barnard, 1982)*
▼

Sex in Samoa – Margaret Mead

The pioneer of gender studies was Margaret Mead (1901–
1978), an American anthropologist and student of Franz
Boas. She did fieldwork on Samoa and Manus (in the
Pacific), with Iatmul and Mundugamor (Papua New
Guinea), on Bali (Indonesia), and with both Native and
Euro-Americans.

Mead was interested in childhood and adolescence, sexuality, and the relation between personality and culture. Her many ethnographies include:

> *Coming of Age in Samoa* (1928)
> *Growing Up in New Guinea* (1930)
> *Sex and Temperament in Three Primitive Societies* (1935).

Mead advocated the use of ethnography in educating the American public about the significance of culture in creating adolescent trauma. Her most famous contribution was her study of adolescent sexuality in Samoa. Supposedly, her Samoan informants did not have adolescent traumas, whereas Americans did. She saw what had formerly been regarded as a universal (adolescent trauma) simply as an aspect of American culture. According to Mead's account, Samoan girls had sex with their boyfriends, and had no guilt feelings or other hang-ups about it. Nor did they have disputes with their parents, who simply turned a blind eye.

In recent years her work has come under fire: apparently her Samoan adolescent female informants told her their sexual fantasies, which she accepted as truth! Derek Freeman's *Margaret Mead and Samoa* (1983) presents this view most strongly. But, for this very reason, her work remains in the forefront of anthropological debate.

Recent interests

Whereas Mead and anthropologists of her time tended to generalise about men and women, or adolescents and adults, today's anthropologists tend to focus on specific members of the communities they work with. Often these people are quoted at length, and thus given the chance to express their own cultural understandings for the anthropological readership. Some of Lila Abu-Lughod's writings on Bedouin women (such as *Veiled Sentiments*, 1986) are good examples.

Such work aims to:

1. allow women to speak for themselves

2. see women as individuals

3. emphasise the complexity of their diverse social roles (for example as sisters, wives, mothers, workers, and community members).

Explaining gender: two views

Anthropologists writing on gender have approached the subject from two points of view. Some see gender mainly as a symbolic construction, while the other sees gender mainly as a set of social relationships.

Figure 29. Woman and man in traditional dress in Sweden (© David Stafford, 1993; courtesy of David Stafford and Jeanne Cannizzo)

Gender as a symbolic construction

Sherry Ortner's 1974 essay 'Is female to male as nature is to culture?' is an example of gender as a symbolic construction. It appeared in *Woman, Culture and Society*, a book edited by Michelle Rosaldo and Louise Lamphere in 1974.

Ortner argues that women everywhere are associated with 'nature'. She says that the biological fact that women, not men, give birth, gives them that universal association. Women's reproductive role tends to confine them to the home. The home, along with women (and to some extent children) represent 'nature' and 'the private', while men represent 'culture' and 'the public'. Ortner does not believe that women are associated with nature in any intrinsic way. Rather, she argues that this cultural universal rests on a symbolic distinction (between nature and culture) found in every society.

Gender as a set of social relationships

Feminists have criticised Ortner's model for not fitting the ethnographic facts. The best-known example is an article by Jane Collier and Michelle Rosaldo, 'Politics and gender in simple societies'. This appeared in a book edited by Sherry Ortner and Harriet Whitehead, *Sexual Meanings: The Cultural Construction of Gender and Sexuality* (1981). Collier and Rosaldo point out that hunting-and-gathering societies in Australia, Africa and the Philippines do not associate childbirth or motherhood with 'nature'. Nor do they associate women simply with reproduction.

Liberating women and men: the feminist critique

The main difference between gender studies and feminist anthropology is that:

1. Gender studies (in its traditional sense) sees gender as an aspect of society, along with economics, politics, and

other perspectives. It sees gender relations as inherent in these other aspects of society. Thus, gender studies might be concerned with the way men and women make a living or how they interact with each other.

2. Feminist anthropology argues that all aspects of society are experienced differently by males and females. Gender becomes central. And the female point of view (otherwise generally ignored) is emphasised.

Female anthropologists have been around for nearly a hundred years. However, through much of the 20th century they did fieldwork as 'honorary males'. Since the 1970s feminist anthropologists started to break down male biases perpetrated even by female anthropologists. Henrietta Moore's book, *Feminism and Anthropology* (1988), gives an excellent discussion of this. Moore emphasises that anthropologists should look at what people (women in particular) say as well as what they do. They should also be aware that women are not the same everywhere, in that what it means to be a woman (or a man) is dependent on culture.

It is not enough simply to talk about being a woman (or a man). An individual is not just 'a woman' but, say, a middle-class, Asian, Muslim woman. The complexities of these roles, taken together, are what makes up her social personality. It is worth adding that a woman is also always a complex of family relations, for she is a wife to one person, a sister to another, and so on. Relations between women and men (or between women and other women, or men and other men) are carried out within families.

One of the most interesting theoretical discussions of modern anthropology is the product of the thinking of a *male* feminist anthropologist. In this book *Blood Relations* (1991), Chris Knight argued that tens of thousand of years ago a sex strike on the part of women, exchanging sex for meat, led to menstrual symbolism and with it, art, religion, and so on. Not everyone who finds this interesting agrees with him, but his book has sparked much debate on the use of comparative ethnography to reconstruct the past and on the 'natural' relation between males and females in human society.

How families and marriage differ in different societies

How families are organised depends in part on what they do. Small family units are common in many industrialised societies. Larger units are common where they are needed for agricultural purposes, such as in India. They are also common where ties between kin provide networks for looking after children; examples include both rural and urban communities.

Different forms of marriage lead to different forms of family organisation. As in the anthropological study of economics (chapter 4), classic examples in the study of the family help us to make key definitions and understand the organising principles of society.

Types of family structure

The most usual classification is as follows:

- *nuclear family* – a married couple and their children; the basic unit of family organization in virtually every society

- *one-parent family* – a variant of the nuclear family; occurs when one parent (usually a woman) raises children on her own; can also be formed through separation, divorce or widowhood

- *compound family* – a central figure (typically a powerful man), his or her spouses, sometimes concubines, and all their children; common in West Africa

- *joint family* – brothers and their wives and children all live together; an effective form of family structure when brothers share property in common, as in parts of India, China and Africa

- *extended family* – an ambiguous term; on the one hand, it means a group of closely-related nuclear families that live together; on the other, it means such a group who don't live together but simply keep in touch (as in newly urban and industrialising societies).

Varieties of marriage

Arguably, marriage exists in every society for two reasons. First it defines the tie between partners. Secondly it legitimates children born to the couple. This doesn't mean that every set of partners gets married, but rather that marriage is defined as the norm and other relationships as more, or less, equivalent to this norm.

One way to classify marriages is according to how many people are involved:

- *monogamy* – marriage to only one other person.

- *polygamy* – marriage to more than one other person. It consists of two forms:

- *polygyny* – one man and more than one woman; common in several parts of the world, notably in traditional African societies.

- *polyandry* – one woman and more than one man, usually a group of brothers; the best-known cases are in South Asia, such as the Todas of India, though the custom is dying out.

- *group marriage* – a hypothetical type; 19th-century anthropologists like Lewis Henry Morgan believed it was a primal type of marriage.

- *gay marriage* – marriage (sometimes called civil partnership) between people of the same sex.

Marrying kinsfolk

It is also possible to classify marriage according to whether the partner is kin or not. When marriage to kinsfolk is the norm, there are two possibilities:

1. To marry 'closely'. This may enable people to be sure of the motives of their spouses, and prevent property from leaving the family. It is common in Arab societies, for example, for a man to marry his father's brother's daughter. She will be known to him since birth, and they will be members of the same kinship group. On the other hand, Trobriand Islanders prefer marriage of a man to his father's sister's daughter, who does not belong to his kinship group.

2. To marry into a permitted category when other categories are expressly forbidden. In various societies in south Asia, south America and Aboriginal Australia, a man may marry a 'cross-cousin' (mother's brother's daughter or father's sister's daughter) but not a 'parallel cousin' (father's brother's daughter or mother's sister's daughter). The reason is that the former are regarded as more distant and the latter too close for marriage. In such societies the latter are regarded as classificatory 'sisters' (see chapter 8).

Figure 30. Man and woman in the Trobriand Islands (© Peter Skalnik, 1988) ▶

Are families and marriage universal?

In his book *Social Structure* (1949), American anthropologist George Peter Murdock argued that the family is universal.

All societies, he said, are organised around either the nuclear family or more complex family structures built upon the nuclear family (compound family, joint family, etc.). However, a number of cases have been suggested which might be problematic for Murdock's notion. The kibbutzim (agricultural communities in which children are raised collectively) of Israel and female-centred families in the West Indies are common examples to suggest that the family, as Murdock understood it, is not universal.

Definition of marriage

The definition of marriage is a related problem. Two well-known cases are the Nayars (a high-status group in South India) and the Lovedu (a South African people).

Example – the Nayars

In the Nayar case, the problem is that marriage entails two separate male roles which, elsewhere in India, are combined. In ordinary, non-Nayar Hindu marriage, the bridegroom ties a tali (the gold emblem which symbolises the union) around the neck of the bride. In Nayar marriage (at least in former times), a high-caste person, often a Brahman, ties the tali. In an Indian context, the ceremony clearly indicates the first stage of a Hindu marriage.

Yet in a worldwide context, the ceremony would seem to resemble more a puberty rite than a marriage, in that it grants the girl full womanhood and enables her to take lovers. The Nayar girl does not sleep with her tali-tier; instead, she takes a series of lovers, called sambandham partners, and they father her children. However, children owe allegiance neither to the man who tied their mother's tali nor to their mother's sambandham partners. Rather, since descent is reckoned matrilineally (see below), they owe allegiance to their mother's brothers.

Example – the Lovedu

The Lovedu represent an example of 'woman marriage'. Since around 1800 the Lovedu have been ruled by a line of biologically female, but socially male women, the remote and mysterious 'rain queens'. Each queen since that time has been married to several other females. Some remain in the royal quarters to be impregnated by male members of the royal house, while others are redistributed to the queen's relatives or other subjects. This pattern maintains alliances between the royal house and the people of scattered localities.

Tutorial

Progress questions

1 What is the difference between sex and gender?

2 Describe the challenge posed by feminist anthropology.

3 Name some of the types of family and marriage structure.

Seminar discussion

Read the ethnographic accounts by Mead (1928) and Freeman (1983) on Samoa. Which view, if either, is correct?

Practical assignments

Look at a discussion of gender in an ethnography of your choice. Think of criticisms which might be raised in light of feminist insights.

Study, revision and exam tips

1 Avoid exclusionist language in your essays and exams. For example, don't say 'we' to refer to females or English people simply because you are female or English. This is off-putting to your reader (who may be neither female nor English).

2 Do memorise lists of things, but also do more than that! Think how they work in practice. Forms of marriage and family organisation are cases in point.

3 Learn specific ethnographic cases to go with anthropological concepts or theoretical points. The Nayar case is a useful example on the concept of 'marriage'.

8 Kinship: Terminology, Descent and Alliance

One-minute overview

Kinship is the most technical branch of anthropology, but it can be fascinating. The key to success to is to learn the basic concepts and master the art of reading and drawing kinship diagrams. Kinship includes the classification of relatives, the formation of kin groups, and aspects of marriage. Anthropologists who emphasise kin groups are called 'descent theorists', and those who emphasise relations between groups (through marriage) are called 'alliance theorists'. In this chapter you will cover:

- ■ 'real' versus 'fictive' kinship
- ■ how to draw kinship diagrams
- ■ how to understand kinship terminologies
- ■ descent theory
- ■ alliance theory
- ■ the new kinship

'Real' versus 'fictive' kinship

There are three main branches in the study of kinship:

1. kinship terminology
2. descent theory
3. alliance theory

Yet the basis of kinship is biology or, some would say, the biological metaphor which defines the subject. The distinction between 'real' and 'fictive' kinship is especially relevant here.

Real kinship

According to conventional understandings in just about all cultures, 'real kinship' entails notions of biology. This sounds straightforward, but there can be problems. What is biology? In a book called *The Sexual Life of Savages* (1929), Malinowski wrote that Trobriand Islanders did not believe that the father had anything to do with conception, which in Trobriand eyes is caused by a spirit of the woman's clan.

Other anthropologists have challenged his interpretation of Trobriand statements on the subject, but his central point still holds: we cannot take for granted that everyone has the same idea of 'biology'. Some argue that the anthropological study of kinship itself is based on Western and not universal ideas of 'biology'. David Schneider (1918–1995) was the leading proponent of this view.

There is, though, a possible way around the problem. Anthropologists often distinguish two kinds of fatherhood and two kinds of motherhood:

- *genitor* – culturally-recognised biological father
- *pater* – social father (including an adoptive father)
- *genetrix* – culturally-recognised biological mother
- *mater* – social mother (including an adoptive mother).

All these relationships imply 'real kinship'.

Figure 31. !Xõo Bushman mother and child (© Alan Barnard, 1982) ◄

Fictive kinship

'Fictive kinship' is, in a strange sense, easier to define than 'real kinship'. It entails relationships which are quite like real kinship ones in some way, but are nevertheless not regarded by the people concerned as really 'real'. Take for example the metaphorical use of kinship terms such as 'sisters' in the feminist movement, priests as 'fathers', or children addressing their parents' friends as, say, 'Auntie Jane' or 'Uncle Charles'. 'Sisters' in the feminist movement have something in common with sisters within a family, but no-one would say that they are exactly the same thing.

Godparenthood and compradrazgo

1. Godparenthood is a common form of 'fictive kinship' found in many Christian cultures. The ritual sponsors of a child at baptism – its 'godparents' – promise to look after the spiritual interests of the child as it grows up. Although a fictive relationship (a godfather is not considered a pater), there are certain elements of the godparent relationship which come close to kinship. For example, in some churches marriage to a godchild or a godparent's child is forbidden. Such rules mimic those of the incest taboo.

2. Compadrazgo is a fictive kin relationship between the godparents of a child and the parents of the child. It is common in certain Roman Catholic societies, notably in Western Mediterranean and Latin American countries. Parents and godparents are said to be campadres (in Spanish). They lend money to each other and generally help out in times of trouble or during religious festivals. Often the compadrazgo relationship is unequal, with the godparents being of higher status than the parents.

How to draw kinship diagrams

Drawing kinship diagrams is something all anthropology students need to know how to do. The principles are very simple:

1. A triangle represents a man (actual or hypothetical).
2. A circle represents a woman.
3. A box or diamond represents a person whose gender is unknown or not relevant (such as a small child).
4. A line above two symbols indicates a sibling relationship (that between brothers and sisters).
5. A line below or an equal sign between two symbols indicates marriage.
6. A dotted or dashed line indicates a sexual relationship other than marriage.
7. A vertical line indicates a parent/child relationship.
8. A line through a symbol indicates a dead person.
9. A line through a horizontal line or equal sign indicates a severed relationship (such as a divorce).

Kinship symbols

In order to describe exact genealogical relationships, anthropologists have invented symbols. The most common system is as follows:

F = father	M = mother	P = parent
B = brother	Z = sister	G = sibling
S = son	D = daughter	C = child
H = husband	W = wife	E = spouse
e = older (elder)	y = younger	
ss = same sex	os = oppostie sex	

The symbols are combined as possessives. For example, FB would mean 'father's brother'. Thus we may say that the English word uncle refers to those who occupy the genealogical positions FB, MB, FZH and MZH. The older/younger and same/opposite-sex distinctions becomes relevant on occasion. A Nharo bushman will distinguish older from younger brothers and sisters. A Trobriand islander will distinguish his or her siblings according to whether they are the same or opposite sex. There is no word in the Trobriand language for 'brother' or 'sister', only words for 'same' or 'opposite-sex siblings' (and younger or older).

Practice

Try describing the relationships shown in the examples of kinship diagrams in figure 32. A and B are identical (man, wife, son and daughter). C shows a woman, her husband and her brother. D shows a woman and her two husbands (one deceased and the other divorced). E shows three generations of individuals related in the male line. F shows an unmarried couple.

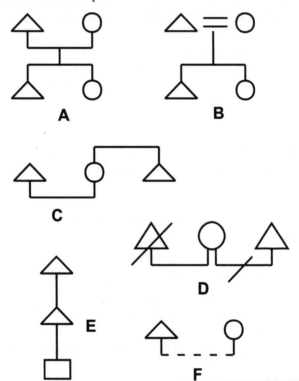

Figure 32. Examples of kinship diagrams. ▶

How to understand kinship terminologies

Purposes of kinship diagrams

Drawing kinship diagrams is one thing. Understanding why to draw them is quite another! Essentially there are two purposes:

1. To illustrate a set relationships, either of real people or of hypothetical ones. Real people would be shown to illustrate someone's actual genealogy. Hypothetical relationships might be diagrammed in order to illustrate some principle, such as descent in the male line (patrilineal descent).

2. To illustrate the structure of a kinship terminology (also called a relationship terminology). It is this one which will concern us here.

Language and terminology

Languages classify the world, and a word in one language will not necessarily have an exact equivalent in another language. Nowhere is this more true than in kinship.

● *Example* – Compare, for example, Latin and English in the classification of 'uncles'. The fact that the Latin language classifies the father's brother (FB) by one term, *patruus*, and the mother's brother (MB) by quite a different one, *avunculus*, gives an indication of the way Roman family life was organised. One's patruus was a stern figure much like the father (*pater*). One's avunculus was literally an 'avuncular' figure, and not a figure of authority.

Anthropologists have devised standard diagrams to illustrate and classify terminologies. There is some debate about the extent to which it is meaningful to classify societies together just because they have the same kinship terminology structure. However, there is general agreement about the patterns into which the world's terminologies fall.

Ensuring comparability

In order to ensure comparability, it is usual to illustrate a terminology structure by showing one – and only one – of each relationship. For example, we need to show one FB and one MB, even though an actual individual might have more than one (or none) of each. We can then see instantly whether FB and MB are called by the same term (as in English) or by two different terms (as in Latin).

The diagrams in figure 33 show the four typical ways of classifying relatives on the generation above one's own and their equivalent ways of classifying relatives of one's own generation. There are six in the latter case, for reasons which will be explained below. The 'self' is conventionally labelled by the Latin term ego (meaning 'I'). For simplicity, the terminology structures are illustrated here with English words. Only the lineal, 'Eskimo' diagram corresponds to actual English usage, and the English terminology itself is of this type.

The simplest type is generational (in terms of the generation above ego) or 'Hawaiian' (in term's of ego's generation). There is no distinction between siblings and cousins. All are termed 'brother' or 'sister'. 'Hawaiian' terminologies are found not only in Hawaii, but also on other parts of Polynesia and commonly in West Africa too.

The so-called 'Eskimo' type is the one found in English-speaking societies, as well as among Inuit or Eskimo groups. It distinguishes siblings from cousins.

Contrast the 'Iroquois' structure, which distinguishes parallel cousins (FBC and MZC) from cross-cousins (FZC and MBC). 'Iroquois' structures are the most common in the world's languages, and are found among Native North American, in many African societies, in some Asian societies, and in Aboriginal Australia. Typically, cross-cousins are people you can marry, whereas parallel cousins are treated as brother and sister. This follows logically from the classification of relatives on the generation above: if you call your FB 'father', it can be expected that you call his children 'brother' and 'sister' (as children of your classificatory 'father').

'Sudanese' terminologies lack generic words altogether. For example, traditional Gaelic-speakers would say mac brathair mathar (literally 'son of the brother of the mother'), since they had no word for 'cousin'. 'Crow' and 'Omaha'

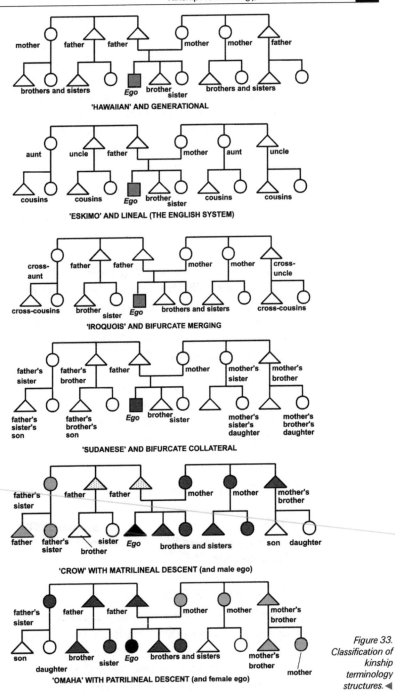

'HAWAIIAN' AND GENERATIONAL

'ESKIMO' AND LINEAL (THE ENGLISH SYSTEM)

'IROQUOIS' AND BIFURCATE MERGING

'SUDANESE' AND BIFURCATE COLLATERAL

'CROW' WITH MATRILINEAL DESCENT (and male ego)

'OMAHA' WITH PATRILINEAL DESCENT (and female ego)

Figure 33.
Classification of
kinship
terminology
structures. ◄

terminologies, common among Native Peoples of the
Americas and in parts of Africa, Asia and the Pacific, imply
strongly matrilineal and patrilineal principles respectively
(see below). The distinguishing feature of 'Crow' is the
classification of a man's FZD as a 'father's sister'; and of
'Omaha', the classification of a woman's MBS as a 'mother's
brother'. The more meaningful way to think of it is that ego
classifies people according to membership in a kin group,
rather than simply by generation.

Study tips for kinship terminologies

Here are some study tips specifically relevant to the study of
kinship terminologies:

1. Take note of what a kinship diagram illustrates. For
   example, does it illustrate a real genealogy, a hypothetical
   genealogy, or a kinship terminology structure? If there is
   exactly one triangle or circle for each genealogical
   position (M, MZ, MB and so on), chances are the
   diagram illustrates a terminology structure.

2. Always draw kinship terminology diagrams in the same
   way unless there is a very good reason not to (e.g. to
   illustrate relative age as a factor in terminology). This is
   essential for making easy comparisons between different
   terminology structures.

3. Typically in a kinship terminology diagram, ego's father is
   on the left and mother on the right, with parallel relatives
   in the middle and cross-relatives on the outside. This
   allows instant recognition of the structure for those who
   know how to read such diagrams.

Descent theory

Descent theory involves the study of group structure and
rules of residence, for example whether upon marriage you
live with the wife's family or with the husband's. It also
involves rules governing the inheritance of property and
succession to title or office, such as a chiefship.

Descent theorists are more concerned with groups than with terminology. Descent theory has always been a major perspective within British anthropology, for example, in the work of A.R. Radcliffe-Brown, Meyer Fortes, and Jack Goody.

Connecting the generations: lines of descent

There are four main types of descent group:

1. patrilineal
2. matrilineal
3. double
4. cognatic or bilateral.

In figure 34, hypothetical patrilineal groups are indicated by number (1 and 2), and matrilineal groups by letter (A and B). Put simply, double descent is patrilineal and matrilineal together, and cognatic or bilateral descent is the absence of either patrilineal or matrilineal groups.

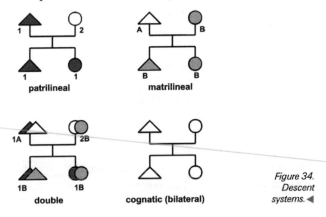

Figure 34.
Descent
systems. ◀

Patrilineal descent

Systems of patrilineal descent are widely distributed throughout the world. The defining characteristic is that group membership is determined by descent through the father. A patrilineal clan will include a person's father, father's father, father's father's father, and so on. The child of any male member of the group, regardless of the child's own sex, is also a member.

Matrilineal descent

Matrilineal descent systems are less common, but are found in Africa, Asia and the Pacific, and in Amerindian societies. Famous examples include the Bemba of Zambia, the Nayars of India, the Trobriand Islanders of Melanesia, and the Iroquois of North America.

Matrilineal descent is defined as descent through the mother. This does not necessarily imply that authority is in the hands of the mother or females generally, but only that one traces membership in the group through female links. Authority within the family may be in the hands of the father, but is more commonly in the hands of the mother's brother. (One's father will be a member of a different matrilineal group, not one's own.) A matrilineal descent group will include a person's mother, mother's mother, mother's mother's mother, and so on, as well as the descendants of all these people in the female line.

Double descent

Double descent is a rare form, where everyone belongs to two kin groups: one patrilineal and the other matrilineal. The best examples are to be found in Africa. The Herero of Namibia are a well-known case. They recognise two distinct sets of unilineal groups. Each Herero belongs both to an oruzo (patrilineal clan) and an eanda (matrilineal clan). Each oruzo is headed by a priest, who distributes property after the death of a member. Fellow oruzo members share food taboos, origin legends, ritual and other activities, and a sacred hearth. One's eanda is less important, but members share similar activities.

Double descent is similar to but distinguished from complementary filiation. 'Complementary filiation' is the term for obligations toward kin on the opposite side of the family from which he or she traces descent.

Cognatic or bilateral descent

This is the opposite of double descent. In a fully cognatic society, there are no patrilineal or matrilineal groups. A person is reckoned to be equally related to kinsfolk on either side of the family. Cognatic kinship is found especially among hunter-gatherers and in technologically-advanced societies. Western societies are mostly cognatic, although surnames and titles of nobility tend to be inherited patrilineally.

Creating groups: residence and descent

Upon marriage, it is usual in almost all societies for a husband and wife to live in the same house. Sometimes, as is usual in Europe, this will be a new home. Often, though, it will be a home in the vicinity of either the husband's family or that of the bride.

Of all the different possibilities of residence, three have a logical tendency to form descent groups.

- *virilocal residence* – residence in the locality of the husband. The consistent practice of virilocal or residence will automatically create groupings of patrilineally-related kin, each residing at the same locality.

- *uxorilocal residence* – residence in the locality of the wife. It keeps matrilineally-related women together and disperses the men. Among the Bemba, it serves the function of permitting a daughter to work the fields she will inherit from her mother.

- *avunculocal residence* – residence with the man's mother's brother (Latin *avunculus*). Among the Trobrianders, each boy leaves his parents' marital home well before the age of marriage in order to live in the village of his mother's brother. He is taught to regard this village as his own because it is the village of his matrilineal kin. A girl will remain in her village of birth until she marries, when she moves away to the villages of her husband (and his brothers and mother's brothers). This practice creates residential units consisting of matrilineally-related men, but disperses the women through whom they are all related. In a matrilineal society it is consistent with keeping power in the hands of men, specifically over their sisters' children (a man's own children will belong to a different matrilineal group).

Alliance theory

Alliance theory is the study of relations between groups, families or individuals through marriage. It originated in France, with Claude Lévi-Strauss's *The Elementary Structures of Kinship* (1949). It is a very prominent theoretical perspective in British anthropology, too. Key figures include Sir Edmund Leach and Rodney Needham.

Incest

Technically, incest is a sexual act between individuals prohibited from engaging in such acts because of their relationship. All societies have incest prohibitions. Many societies classify everyone as 'kin', and also have categories of kin with whom it is especially permissible to engage in sex and to marry. Alliance theorists tend to be most interested in these societies. They reject the idea that group membership is what creates society. Rather they see society in terms of links between intermarrying groups.

Elementary structures of kinship

Elementary structures involve patterns established by positive rules of marriage which are sort of the opposite of an incest taboo: not 'You cannot marry your sister', but 'You must marry someone you call 'cross-cousin'.' What Lévi-Strauss called complex structures are those with negative rules: 'You cannot marry your sister'. The latter are of less interest because they do not create patterns of relations between kin groups. Lévi-Strauss has claimed that elementary structures represent the earliest forms of human kinship, and the ones which are fundamental to understanding the meaning of the incest taboo.

There are three forms of elementary structure. Try drawing diagrams of the relevant marriages, repeated through the generations, and see how they work.

- *Generalised exchange* (figure 35) – Group A gives its women as wives to group B, who give theirs to group C, and so on. Consistent with a pattern of marriages of men to their mothers' brothers' daughters (MBDs). This tends to involve a hierarchical relation between groups: for example, if a man takes a wife from the same group as his father, and men always owe deference to those from whom they receive their wives. Common in southeast Asia. Famous examples include Kachin (studied by Leach) and Purum (described by Needham).

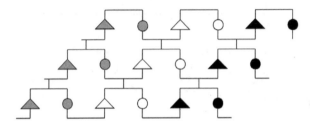

Figure 35. Generalised exchange (idealised model, with three patrilineal groups) ◄

- *Delayed restricted (or delayed direct) exchange* (figure 36) – Group A gives women to group B, and B to C in one generation, then each group receives women back in the next generation. Consistent with a pattern of marriages of men to their fathers' sisters' daughters (FZDs). Very rare, as it establishes no consistent relationship between groups and thus tends to break down. Some anthropologists claim it exists only as a theoretical type.

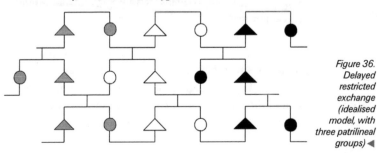

Figure 36. Delayed restricted exchange (idealised model, with three patrilineal groups) ◄

- *Restricted (or direct) exchange* (figure 37) – Group A gives women to group B, and group B gives women to group A. Consistent with a pattern of marriages permitted to either mothers' brothers' daughters (MBDs) or fathers' sisters' daughters (FZDs). Often found in societies where there are just two descent groups (in which case they are called moieties): one's own moiety (including one's brothers and sisters and parallel cousins), and the moiety one marries into (including one's cross-cousins). Common in Amazonia, south Asia and Aboriginal Australia.

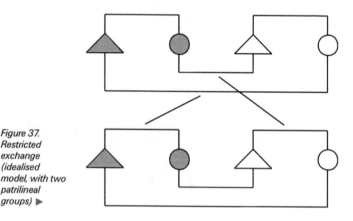

Figure 37. Restricted exchange (idealised model, with two patrilineal groups) ▶

The Crow-Omaha system

Finally, Lévi-Strauss and his followers recognise a type of system which lies between elementary and complex. This is a Crow-Omaha system. Such systems include most (but not all) those with 'Crow' or 'Omaha' kinship terminologies.

In general, 'Crow' or 'Omaha' terminologies define whom one cannot marry: anyone called by the same kinship term as a close relative. This entails a negative marriage rule, and therefore a complex structure. But there are so many prohibitions that these systems come to resemble elementary structures. From an individual (though not a group) point of view, they are similar to systems of generalised exchange in the way they limit the choice of spouse.

The new kinship

As early as the 1960s there were attempts to get away from classic interests in kinship structures. Some anthropologists felt that while many African peoples were ideally studied through descent theory and South American and Australian people through alliance theory, these perspectives lacked something more general.

This was shown especially by David Schneider's studies of the inhabitants of the island of Yap in the Pacific and middle class Americans of Chicago. Schneider focused on such things as the symbolism of kinship by 'blood' among Americans, for example in his book *American Kinship* (first edition, 1968).

Related and more recent anthropological interests have included the study of adoption and fostering and new reproductive technologies, such as in vitro fertilisation. Such technological developments challenge the formerly more clear-cut distinction between biological and social kinship. In her recent book *After Kinship* (2004), Janet Carsten explores these issues cross-culturally, as well as the relation between kinship and such things as gender, the body, the house, and the nation. Many anthropologists feel these things will become more prominent in kinship studies in the future.

Tutorial

Progress questions

1 How can 'real' kinship be distinguished from 'fictive' kinship?

2 Diagram and describe some of the different kinds of kinship terminology. How do they differ from one another?

3 What is the debate between descent theory and alliance theory all about?

4 What is new about the 'new kinship'?

Seminar discussion

Different peoples have different ways of classifying relatives. Might this mean that they perceive biological relationships differently?

Practical assignment

Draw your own genealogy. Note which ancestors are known to you and which are not, and why. For example, is there a patrilineal bias in your family's memory? Is there an emphasis on ancestors who lived a long time, who did something important, or who lived in your area? Now note which relatives of your own generation you have included: brothers and sisters, first cousins, second cousins, etc. Any biases here?

Study, revision and exam tips

1. When studying a kinship system very different from your own, try to think like a member of the society you are studying.

2. Whenever you find a list of kinship terms in an ethnography, draw a kinship diagram to help you visualise the structure.

3. Many students find kinship difficult. When revising for exams, don't feel put off if you have difficulty remembering all the details. Rather, think about what you do know. By the same reasoning, when going through previous exam papers it is often best to concentrate on questions you can answer rather than those you can't.

9 | **Applied and Development Anthropology**

One-minute overview

Some anthropologists regard applied anthropology as a
branch of anthropology concerned with practical problems,
while others believe that all anthropology has the potential
for application. Whatever their point of view, those who
practise applied anthropology use anthropological ideas in
areas like multicultural education, government, medicine or
charity work. Development anthropology is a related field.
Development anthropologists concentrate on advising
governments and charities on social and cultural aspects of
economic development, especially in the Third World. In
this chapter you will cover:

- what is applied anthropology?
- understanding 'self' and 'other'
- putting theory into practice
- anthropology in policy and action
- social development in the Third World
- retaining cultural values

What is applied anthropology?

'Applied anthropology' means different things to different
people. To some (especially in North America) it is a
specialisation or even a distinct branch of anthropology.
There is a journal devoted to applied work called *Human
Organization*, most of whose contributors seem to subscribe
to this view.

The alternative regards all anthropology as 'applied', as
anthropology itself highlights social issues and aids human
understanding. The pure/applied distinction is, in other

words, less clear in anthropology than in the natural sciences.

Understanding 'self' and 'other'

Avoiding ethnocentrism

Ethnocentrism is when one assumes erroneously that another culture is like one's own. By learning about other cultures in a systematic way, we develop an awareness of cultural differences and a tolerance for other cultures. This enables us to avoid wrongful, ethnocentric visions of people who differ from ourselves. This can be especially important in mutlicultural societies such as the UK, where cultures come into contact.

Cultural difference can be pronounced, or it can be quite subtle. There are cultural differences which have the potential of negative, ethnocentric feelings between, for example, Britons and Americans.

In the 1940s British anthropologist Gregory Bateson (who is married to an American anthropologist) argued that there are cultural reasons why Britons think Americans are boastful and Americans think Britons are arrogant.

(a) In America, he said, children are encouraged to do most of the talking while adults listen; therefore in America to do all the talking is polite (equated with subordinate, childlike) behaviour.

(b) In Britain the reverse is true; thus to talk about oneself (as Americans often do) is seen in Britain as boastful. Americans see the British propensity not to talk about oneself as arrogant, since they see this silence as an impolite, domineering attempt to listen when a polite person should be speaking!

Putting theory into practice

Spheres of exchange and the arrival of money

In chapter 4 we learned about 'spheres of exchange', a theoretical notion which is used in economic anthropology. Consider now the case of the Tiv, an agricultural people of eastern Nigeria.

The Tiv of Nigeria

Traditionally they had three spheres, though these were somewhat disrupted during British colonial rule.

1. The most prestigious sphere was that of rights in human beings, especially women 'exchanged' for other women in arranged marriages.

2. The second, also a prestige sphere, was that of slaves, cattle, cloth and metal bars.

3. The third was of food and of utilitarian goods: mortars, grindstones, calabashes, baskets, pots, etc., and also live chickens and goats.

Tiv understood these exchanges in terms of 'buying' and 'selling', in the sense that in any given exchange one party was considered the 'buyer' and the other the 'seller'. They also distinguished them sharply from gift-giving: their market (buying and selling) relationships were immediate, whereas gift-giving ones were built up over time. Furthermore, prices could vary within a sphere (today a cow might be worth ten pieces of cloth, tomorrow nine pieces of cloth).

In principle, the spheres were separate. However, they were not as separate as those of the Trobrianders. When a Tiv family fell on hard times, they might be tempted to exchange across the spheres. Doing this, though, entailed a severe loss of face on the part of those seeking goods 'down' the spheres, and a comparable gain in status of those going 'up'. If a man had to sell his cow for pots and pans he might become richer in low-status goods, but he would lose status as a result.

The colonial officials did not understand the system. They thought that brass rods being exchanged in the second sphere were Tiv 'money', and in the 1950s tried to set a value for them in the coin of the realm. This was a problem because British money could be exchanged in the third sphere for low-status goods. Thus the British, without realizing it, disrupted the Tiv economy.

Paul and Laura Bohannan, anthropologists working with the Tiv, noted the problem and called attention to it. However, their discoveries were too late for the colonial administrators or subsequent governments to intervene. The Bohannans wrote a book called *Tiv Economy* (1968), as well as other works pointing out the problematic nature of economic intervention. Had colonial officials been able to draw on their work, things might have gone better for the Tiv and their transition to the world economy.

Prospects for applied work

The Tiv case is a famous one, but it is by no means unique. Anthropologists today are employed by governments, especially in rural development in the Third World, to advise on potential problems of modernization. Anthropologists, with their knowledge of traditional forms of kinship, religious belief, politics and economics, are in a unique position to identify pitfalls in planned and unplanned change.

Nor is it only in the Third World that applied work is an issue. In North America, there are many practising anthropologists who use their general knowledge of cultures to help solve problems due to cultural misunderstanding. The practice is growing in the UK too, and new specialisms are emerging. For example, British anthropologist Anthony Good who previously studied kinship and religion in South

Asia has become a specialist in court procedure relating to the seeking of refugee status on the part of Sri Lankans who have come to the UK.

Using anthropology in policy and action

Using anthropology to influence government policy

The peoples anthropologists work with are often poor and marginalized. Some are the subject of political discrimination too.

In South Africa during the apartheid era, many anthropologists were active opponents of their government. They tried to show the ways in which South African society itself was economically and socially integrated, and therefore the fallacy of the government's idea of 'separate development'. In post-apartheid South Africa, anthropologists are helping to understand the effects of separation of migrant labourers from their families, the day-to-day activities of people still trying to cope with poverty, and changing notions of social identity. These understandings will, it is hoped, help the very individuals who have been objects of anthropological study.

*Figure 38.
Children with T-
shirts
celebrating ten
years of free
elections in
post-apartheid
South Africa
(© Alan
Barnard,
2004)* ◄

In Australia, Canada, Brazil and other countries, anthropologists are active in the struggles for the rights of indigenous peoples. The major issue is land rights. Through in-depth studies of the ways in which people use and appreciate the land, anthropologists have been able to show that land is not simply a commodity to be bought or sold. It is the essence of their identity in many cases.

Australian Aborigines, for example, believe that their clans originated at specific places which they designate as sacred sites. Applied anthropologists have helped Aborigines document claims to these sites and the lands which surround them. Such claims have been the subject of numerous legal actions. Several cases are described in Kenneth Maddock's important book, *Your Land is Our Land* (1983). Examples of similar cases in Australia and other countries may be found in *We are Here: Politics of Aboriginal Land Tenure* (1989), a book of essays edited by Edwin Wilmsen.

Using anthropology in medicine

Medical anthropology is a rapidly growing field and an excellent example of how anthropological knowledge can be put into action for the benefit of either a specific community or for society as a whole.

Medical anthropologists generally accept the existence of universal principles in medicine (what anthropologists in general call the **etic** framework), but they tend to be more interested in the particular ways of thinking characteristic of specific cultures (the **emic** framework). Cecil Helman's book, *Culture, Health and Illness* (fourth edition, 2001), reports on hundreds of studies to illustrate the cultural as well as the biological foundations of stress, pain, psychological disorders, and the definitions of various illnesses. For instance, North American psychiatrists are more prone to diagnosing 'schizophrenia' than those in Britain. Similarly, a North American doctor will diagnose 'emphysema' where a British doctor reads the same symptoms as 'chronic bronchitis'.

This doesn't mean that modern medicine is fallacious, but that culture is everywhere, even in medical science. Helman himself is a practising physician as well as a medical anthropologist, and his book is intended mainly for health professionals.

Common activities of medical anthropologists

(a) learning the cultural basis of health and illness

(b) educating medical people about cultural awareness

(c) helping medical practitioners to solve problems related to cultural awareness and relationships with patients

(d) studying and understanding doctor/patient relationships in general.

The kinds of cultural factors appropriate for such studies include family structures, gender roles, sexual behaviour, beliefs about procreation and contraception, diet and body image, personal hygiene, religion, and many others. Anthropologists today are also greatly involved in the study of HIV/AIDS and even in issues such as organ donation and sale.

Social development in the Third World

The notion of 'development' was conceived in the 1940s. At that time the concept was essentially global rather than local, and local customs were frequently regarded as causing people to remain 'backward'. Most anthropologists believe that such negative views are inappropriate, and that real development can only be achieved through an appreciation of cultural diversity. Anthropologists in development work emphasize people-centred approaches, which make local conditions, local needs, and cultural perceptions central to development practice.

Projects and programmes

Historically, development theory has moved from large-scale

economic development concerns to small-scale, project-based ones. The integration of social as well as economic facts in development has (like the substantivist approach in economic anthropology) led to a greater emphasis on culture as a determinant factor.

It is important in development work to distinguish between a project and a programme. A **project** is a small-scale activity; a **programme** is a large-scale activity which may include several projects. Anthropologists tend to be active more at project level, either to implement projects or to advise governments or non-governmental organizations (charities) on relevant social and cultural issues.

Examples

Examples of development ideas which anthropologists may be involved in include:

(a) agricultural improvement
(b) indigenous knowledge
(c) urban regeneration
(d) empowerment (giving ordinary, especially poor people, power to change their own lives for the better)

Take the first example. Agricultural improvement is not the same things as increasing crop yield. It also entails making sure changes in agriculture fit with the cultural background and current social situation.

Another dimension is indigenous knowledge. It is not uncommon that indigenous peoples have a great knowledge of what plants will grow in particular circumstances and which ones will not. Anthropologists can act as mediators between indigenous groups and outside 'experts'. Urban regeneration and empowerment are topical issues. Projects designed to help street children in urban areas of South Africa, Brazil and India, for example may involve both these issues.

More detail on how anthropologists can help in development projects and programmes may be found in the many books now available on aspects of anthropology and development. Neil Thin, for example, who has experience in India, Indonesia, and Rwanda, uses these to good effect both as a development practitioner and in background for his book *Social Progress and Sustainable Development* (2002). Another interesting, if unusual, use of anthropology in development is shown in David Mosse's book *Cultivating Development: An Ethnography of Aid Policy and Practice* (2005), which is an ethnographic study of the development community itself: specifically of a case in India where the development process did not go quite according to plan. Mosse argues that development practice is driven not so much by policy as by the need for development organizations to maintain relations within the communities in which they work.

Appropriate technology

Technology may be defined as the knowledge of arts and skills needed to make tools and other useful objects. Outside of anthropology, people tend to think of the word as referring mainly to 'advanced technology', such as computers. Yet anthropologists more often think in terms of simpler technologies, such as the bow and arrow, clay pottery, or irrigation systems.

Technology enables people to make efficient use of their respective environments. As technological efficiency increases, society changes. Although there is no universally-applicable correlation between specific technologies and specific forms of society, the interplay between technology and society is a subject of significant interest. Indeed, First as well as Third World societies also have need of appropriate technology (see figure 39).

The use of technology must be appropriate in the sense that it is:

Figure 39. Urban rice farming in the First World: Osaka, Japan (© Alan Barnard, 1988) ▶

- technically achievable

- appropriate to the social circumstances (and not disruptive to them)

- sustainable (capable of being maintained without further intervention).

Not all development projects fulfil these criteria. A project involving the building of a dam to provide electricity may be damaging in that it can cause flooding detrimental to the land-based subsistence of the people it is trying to help. This situation is more common than one might imagine, but happily, anthropologists today are often in a position to point out such problems.

Rethinking cultural values

On a deeper level, some anthropologists have challenged the idea of development as always a good thing. In the 1992 American television series *Millennium* (1992) and the book of the same name, anthropologist David Maybury-Lewis denied both the inevitability and the desirability of full modernisantion.

Consider for example that in traditional societies (as Maybury-Lewis called them) trade is based not just on economic rationality but on social relations. This was part of the argument of the substantivists in economic anthropology. Traditional societies see people and social relationships as central, whereas modern societies emphasise individualism and the relation between individuals and property. Traditional societies have a highly developed sense of community and of spirituality, and modern societies are characterised instead by alienation.

Finding a way to help people achieve material goals while at the same time preserving the best in their society is often a major task of the development anthropologist. It is also a difficult task.

Tutorial

Progress questions

1. What is applied anthropology?

2. How can anthropology be useful in public policy? In medicine?

3. What is the difference between a development project and a development programme?

4. How can anthropology help to alleviate the ill effects of modernisation?

Seminar discussion

Consider the proposition that: 'All anthropology is applied, because there is an anthropological way of looking at the world which renders the world's problems easier to understand.'

Practical assignment

Practise using appropriate behaviour for another culture with your classmates. The heightened awareness of cultural difference is very much part of anthropology, especially in fieldwork.

Study, revision and exam tips

1 When you read texts in 'pure' anthropology, consider also their applied aspects. This may help, for example, in discussing questions like the seminar discussion question posed above.

2 Observe customs as you study them. Try to integrate the book-knowledge of your course with your own observations of cultural differences.

3 Use what you learn as you learn it. For example, when you read an ethnography try to put yourself in the position of someone able to advise on policy issues.

Anthropological theory

Anthropological theory both guides anthropological research and gives meaning to its findings. It provides a framework for the understanding of culture and society. Because anthropologists have different views on how such a framework should be constructed, they are frequently in debate. Anthropological theory has changed greatly over the years, but many anthropologists hold onto older ideas or define their present position according to important debates of the past. In this chapter you will cover:

- why theory is important
- is humankind inventive or not?: evolution vs diffusion
- culture and personality
- functionalism: finding purpose in social organization
- structuralism: finding meaning in relations between things
- anthropology as 'cultural translation'
- anthropology as 'a kind of writing'
- ideas from outside anthropology
- using theory in your essays and exams

Why theory is important

Along with fieldwork, theory is at the heart of anthropology. We have met theoretical issues already. In chapter 4, for example, we saw how the debate between the formalists and substantivists, and later the Marxists, set the direction for economic anthropology. In chapter 8 we saw the importance of the debate between descent theory and alliance theory in the understanding of kinship.

The issues of concern in this chapter are the ones that go beyond subdisciplinary areas like economics or kinship. Sometimes these issues are referred to collectively as 'grand theory'. Grand theory is important for several reasons:

1. It allows us to focus on big questions, like the relation between the individual and society, or how and why societies change.

2. It provides distinctly anthropological understandings which may contribute to interdisciplinary questions, such as those which link anthropology to psychology, sociology, or development studies.

3. It bridges the boundaries of subdisciplines within anthropology.

4. It gives purpose to ethnography.

Focusing on really big questions

Like all disciplines, social anthropology has purpose. At least one of its purposes is to make sense of human society and social action cross-culturally. Anthropologists may look at similar questions to those posed by practitioners of other disciplines, but they approach the questions with a greater emphasis on similarities and differences between cultures.

Think about how societies change. Do they evolve from simple to complex? Or is it rather the passing of material goods, new inventions, or new ways of thinking from one society to the next which is important?

Providing distinctly anthropological understandings

Anthropologists may ask similar questions as those posed by practitioners of other disciplines. Yet the anthropological outlook is different because of its emphasis on cross-cultural understandings.

Therefore anthropologists can provide insights to:

(a) philosophers looking at ways of thinking

(b) archaeologists interested in questions of evolution

(c) psychologists toying with what is human and what is cultural in their understandings of processes of thought

(d) development experts trying to find a way forward for
   projects dependent on social relevance.

Bridging the boundaries of the subdisciplines

All social anthropologists specialize. Nobody can claim equal
expertise in all branches of the subject. Anthropological
theory can pull together interests which lie across the
boundaries of the subdisciplines and provide a focus for
social anthropology as a whole.

Giving purpose to ethnography

Anthropological theory gives purpose to ethnography by
providing questions both when in the field and when the
anthropologist returns and compares results with others.
When in the field, an anthropologist may wish to emphasize
how aspects of society fit together, or simply how she relates
to her informants and they to each other. When she gets
home, she will compare her results to those of others. Do
diverse findings imply a difference in time between an
earlier ethnography? A difference in place? Or just different
perspectives among ethnographers?

Question – Can ethnography exist independently to theory?

Answer – Many anthropologists subscribe to the view that
ethnography cannot exist without theory. By this they mean
that without a perspective about what is and what isn't
important, there is nothing to choose between writing down
one fact and writing down another. Facts take on their
meaning in relation to each other. It is by making
generalizations that we make progress.

Example: generalisations about gender roles
For example, we make generalizations about gender roles in
a particular society on the basis of facts collected about
individuals. We then compare these generalizations to
similar ones made by other ethnographers on other
societies. We might make further generalizations, say, on the

relation between gender and political structure. Are male and female roles perceived differently in hierarchical and egalitarian societies? How does economy affect things? Does it matter whether it is men or women who are most responsible for subsistence?

Ethnography and theory depend on each other, and together give purpose to anthropology. This chapter deals with six major theoretical perspectives. Fig. 11. shows a time line of the duration of these perspectives.

Fig. 40. A time line of theoretical perspectives ▼

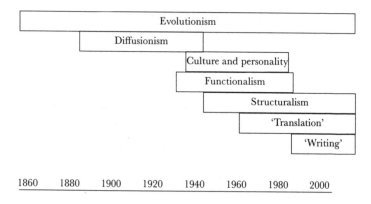

Is humankind inventive or not? Evolution versus diffusion

Do you think human beings are inventive? If so, how many times will the same thing be invented? Or do you think human beings are uninventive? If so, how far do you think something (like pottery-making skills, or the bow and arrow) might have travelled before the global communication system we have today? These are the sorts of grand questions which have engaged evolutionists and diffusionists.

Understanding evolutionism

Evolutionists are those interested in how cultures and societies change and develop from simple to complex. The evolutionist perspective was most prominent in the late 19th century, but it returned to popularity in the late 20th century.

Evolutionism presupposes the following:

(a) Humankind is basically inventive.

(b) Therefore one idea, procedure or tool may be invented more than once.

(c) Humans everywhere think in much the same way (the 'psychic unity' of humankind).

(d) Therefore the same things will be invented in different places across the globe.

That said, evolutionists disagree on the importance of local differences and historical processes. Evolutionists can be divided into four camps:

- *Unilinear evolutionists* (from the mid 19th century) hold that there is a precise line of evolution, the same everywhere. For example, according to Sir John Lubbock (1834–1913), religion evolved from atheism to fetishism to nature-worship or totemism to shamanism to idolotry to theism.

- *Universal evolutionists* (from the early 20th century) hold that only general trends are the same everywhere. Archaeologist V. Gordon Childe (1892-1957) traced evolution from hunting and gathering to agriculture, to the formation of states; and from the urban revolution to the 'revolution in human knowledge' since the invention of writing.

- *Multilinear evolutionists* (from the mid 20th century) hold that there are many lines of evolution. Local history and ecological constraints create different evolutionary paths in different parts of the world. For example Julian Steward (1902–1972) emphasized the role of the environment in the evolution of specific hunting-and-gathering societies.

- *Sociobiologists* (from the late 20th century) hold that human social evolution is similar to that of animals. For example, Robin Fox (1934–) argues that the rudiments of human kinship can be found in primate societies.

Understanding diffusionism

Diffusionists presuppose the following:

(a) Humankind is basically uninventive.

(b) Therefore ideas, procedures or tools tend to be invented only once or twice.

(c) Thus, when similar ones are found in different parts of the world, we must assume that they passed from one place to another.

(d) Things travel either by diffusion proper (the thing passes from one people to another) or by migration of entire populations.

There were two main schools of diffusionism:

1. German-Austrian diffusionists (early 20th century) were interested in waves of diffusion, or what they called 'culture circles'. According to Leo Frobenius (1873–1938), bow-and-arrow culture spread through the world, supplanting spear culture.

2. British diffusionists (early 20th century) were more extreme than the Germans and Austrians. They held that virtually all culture originated in Ancient Egypt and spread from there to the rest of the world. William James Perry (1887–1949) tried to trace the spread of sun-worship and burial pyramids from Egypt to other parts of the world.

Pros and cons of evolutionism and diffusionism

Pros
- They seek origins.
- They take account of history.

Cons
- They emphasize the past over the present.
- Most of their suppositions are untestable and their assertions unreliable.

Culture and personality

By the 1920s anthropologists were beginning to reject evolutionism and diffusionism. Many felt these approaches neglected everyday life. One school which emerged was that of culture and personality. The classic text remains *Patterns of Culture* (1934) by Ruth Benedict (1887–1948). The gist of the book is the comparison of three cultures:

1. Zuñi (New Mexico). They live an ordered life. They are very concerned with obeying rules of behaviour.

2. Kwakiutl (British Columbia). They take everything to extremes. In their potlatches they give away their wealth and destroy it (see Chapter 4).

3. Dobuans (Papua New Guinea). Hostility and fear are normal, and treachery is common. Dobuans are well known for practising sorcery against other members of their community.

The point of Benedict's examples is that what is normal in one culture may not be normal in another. In psychiatric terms, the extremes of behaviour exhibited may be regarded respectively as neurotic (Zuñi), megalomanic (Kwakiutl) and paranoid (Dobuan).

Pros and cons of the 'culture and personality' approach

Pros

- Cultures are understood as wholes.
- Whole cultures can be compared.

Cons

- There is a tendency to stereotype cultures.
- Comparison may end up too simplistic.

Functionalism: finding purpose in social organisation

Functionalism dates from the 1920s. It is concerned with finding (a) reasons why people act the way they do and (b) interrelations between different aspects of society. Whereas personality was mainly an American interest, functionalism was predominantly a British focus. The leaders of functionalist anthropology were Bronislaw Malinowski and A.R. Radcliffe-Brown.

Malinowski

Bronislaw Malinowski was a pioneer of modern fieldwork methods (see chapter 2). He emphasized functional relations which ethnographers could observe in the field. He also tried to emphasize relations between biological needs and cultural life.

Radcliffe-Brown

A.R. Radcliffe-Brown (1881–1955) emphasized the interrelation between social systems: kinship, politics, economics and religion. He was also interested in the function of social institutions (e.g., marriage, initiation) within these systems. Above all, he believed the goal of anthropology ought to be the comparison of societies and formulation of general laws to explain how society works. Sometimes Radcliffe-Brown's approach is referred to as

Figure 41. Bronislaw Malinowski, 1942 ◄

Figure 42. A.R. Radcliffe-Brown (then known simply as Alfred or 'Rex' Brown), 1909 ►

structural-functionalism and Malinowski's as (pure) functionalism.

Pros and cons of functionalism

Pros

- The approach is an excellent one for fieldwork.
- It is based on common sense.

Cons

- The approach is too static; it underestimates cultural change.
- Radcliffe-Brown's general laws of society remain elusive.

Structuralism: finding meaning in relations between things

Structuralism is the perspective which argues that meaning is only revealed through the relation between things. Things have no meaning independently. This perspective was borrowed from linguistics and developed by French anthropologist Claude Lévi-Strauss (1908–) and his British admirers such as Sir Edmund Leach (1910–1989).

In rituals meaning is embedded in the juxtaposition of ritual actions. In mythology meaning is found in contrasts between events or between characters (see Chapter 6).

Example – Colours take on meaning in relation to other colours within certain cultural contexts. Red in contrast to green and amber (in a traffic light) means 'stop', while red in contrast to blue or yellow (on a politician's rosette) means 'Labour Party'. These are relatively trivial, if easy to understand, cases. Structuralists studying myth and symbolism use very similar methods to tease out meanings in much deeper realms of culture.

Pros and cons of structuralism

Pros

- Structuralism uncovers deep, sometimes subconscious meanings.
- The approach can be applied in almost any realm of culture.

Cons

- Structuralism cannot explain the richness of culture.
- It de-emphasizes the role of the individual.

Anthropology as 'cultural translation'

Structuralism treats culture 'like a language' to be understood as possessing a 'grammar'. The anthropologist figures out the 'grammar' which relates one element of culture to another.

Yet another approach treats culture as 'like a language', but in quite a different sense. This is the idea of anthropology as 'translation'. The anthropologist learns the cultural 'language' and translates it into terms understandable in his of her own culture. Examples include Evans-Pritchard's *Nuer Religion* (1956) and the essays which make up Clifford Geertz's *The Interpretation of Cultures* (1973).

However, such approaches are not without critics. British anthropologist Adam Kuper, in his book *Culture: The*

Anthropologists' Account (1999), has attacked the very idea of emphasising culture and cultural translation, especially in American anthropology.

Pros and cons of anthropology as 'translation'

Pros
- The aim is to capture the essence of a culture.
- The approach emphasizes feelings and is especially appropriate for the study of things like religious belief.

Cons
- Critics (such as structuralists) claim the essence of a culture cannot be understood without understanding the relations between the elements.
- No translation is ever perfect, either a linguistic one or a (metaphorical) cultural one. Too literal and it becomes unintelligible in the recipient language or culture. Too idiomatic and it fails to capture the true meaning of the original.

Figure 43. Anthropologists from Britain, Tanzania, the United States and Canada debating at a conference in Osaka, Japan (© Joy Barnard, 1998) ◄

Anthropology as 'a kind of writing'

Clifford Geertz (1926–) has been responsible for another theoretical development. He emphasizes not only the idea of 'translation' but also the idea of ethnographic writing as a genre within literature.

A key concept in this approach is thick description. Good ethnographic writing included 'thick' layers of description of many kinds: ethnographic details, different informants' interpretations, the ethnographer's interpretation, etc. The approach has been taken to an extreme in the work of some of Geertz's followers. The most famous case is that of the collection *Writing Culture* (1986) edited by James Clifford and George E. Marcus.

Pros and cons of anthropology as 'writing'

Pros
- Geertz's emphasis has led to a greater awareness of good (and bad) writing in anthropology.
- *Writing Culture* sparked much debate on the creative role of the anthropologist as a writer.

Cons
- Too much emphasis on the anthropologist obscures the importance of the people and society under study.
- Thick description is no substitute for comparison.

Ideas from outside anthropology

There is a trend today to borrow ideas from outside anthropology. Anthropologists have long looked to sociology and to linguistics for ideas, but now too many pick up ideas from fields as diverse as literary criticism, philosophy, and political theory.

One common idea now is that of 'discourse', as used by the French philosopher Michel Foucault (1926–1984). This entails a way of talking, but in Foucault's usage it also implies knowledge and power built into the framework of the 'discourse'. Anthropologists influenced by Foucault sometimes replace the old idea of culture with the idea of discourse and its added implication that powerful groups may through discourse exercise control over less powerful groups.

The existence of such ideas from other disciplines highlights the fact that anthropology is not a closed system. It has links to many fields, and can be enlightened by them. Especially powerful now are ideas from 'postmodernism', which emphasises the partial nature of knowledge and rejects grand theories like evolutionism or structuralism.

There is no agreement though on anthropology's future direction. Robert Layton in *An Introduction to Theory in Anthropology* (1997) tells us that anthropology is split between old-style ecological anthropologists (whose ideas grew from evolutionism) and new-style postmodernists. Which way it goes will depend on the next generation.

Using theory in your essays and exams

As with ethnography (chapter 2), it is almost always an advantage to use theory in your essays and exams. To use theory well:

1. Consider if the question itself presupposes a particular theoretical point of view. Is your tutor trying to get you to agree or disagree with a particular approach?

2. Consider the wider picture. Would mention of major theorists be an advantage? Often it is, but make sure they are relevant to the question and to the perspective you take in your answer.

3. Where appropriate, make your own theoretical perspective clear. The examples in this chapter cover most major or 'grand' perspectives. Other perspectives, often geared towards more particular problems, are found throughout this book.

Tutorial

Progress questions

1 Why do anthropologists put such an emphasis on theory?

2 What are the main theoretical perspectives in anthropology?

3 Which perspectives are now current? Which ones were prominent in the past?

Seminar discussion

Consider the 'Pros and cons' sections of this chapter. Debate the pros and cons of one or more theoretical perspectives with your classmates.

Practical assignment

Read a theoretical text, old or recent, and write a book review of it. Before you start, look at book reviews in journals such as *Social Anthropology, The Journal of the Royal Anthropological Institute* or *American Anthropologist*. Make sure your review includes both a summary and some critical discussion of the book.

Study, revision and exam tips

1 Read theoretical works in conjunction with ethnographies, for example, an ethnography by Malinowski and one of his more theoretical works.

2 Ask yourself whether there might be more than one point of view on a particular topic. Look for evidence for each point of view. Compare the views of different anthropologists when they disagree.

3 Where possible, use quotations in essays and exams. But don't use too many, and *always* make clear that they are quotations and not your own work. Keep them short, and aim for ones that express a definite theoretical position and are not merely descriptive.

4   Reflect on why you chose to study Social Anthropology.
Were you hoping to answer any 'really big questions'? If
your answer is 'yes', this may help you to understand the
reason why anthropology has developed the theories it
has.

Glossary

acephalous Literally 'headless', without leaders.

adaptation The ability of a people to respond favourably to environmental stress.

alliance theory In kinship, the perspective which involves the study of relations between groups through marriage. Alliance theorists are especially interested in the social effects of repeated intermarriages between groups.

animism A belief in a spiritual presence within things such as rocks and trees.

anthropology In its widest sense, the subject which includes social or cultural anthropology, anthropological linguistics, prehistoric archaeology, and biological or physical anthropology. In a narrower sense, a short name for social anthropology.

applied anthropology The branch of anthropology concerned with practical problems. Some anthropologists believe that all anthropology has the potential for application.

articulation of modes of production The interaction between different modes of production, as when a capitalist society comes into contact with a hunting-and-gathering one.

'big man' system A form of political organization in which men gain power by being involved in economic transactions, collecting and redistributing wealth. These are common in Melanesia.

bilateral descent A synonym for cognatic descent.

cargo cult A religious cult formed around the idea that at the dawn of a new age the ancestors will return with a cargo of valuable goods. Such cults have been common in Melanesia.

carrying capacity The maximum number of people who can live in a given environment.

clan A patrilineal or matrilineal kin group tracing descent from a common ancestor, but not knowing their exact relationship to every other clan member (contrast 'lineage').

cognatic descent Descent from both sides of the family equally. In cognatic descent, there are no clans or lineages. This is the opposite of double descent, where people belong to both matrilineal and patrilineal groups at the same time.

communitas Victor Turner's term for an unstructured realm of society, where often the normal ranking of individuals is reversed or the symbols of rank inverted. This sense of 'community' characterizes rites of passage.

compadrazgo A fictive kin relationship between the godparents of a child and the parents of the child. It is common in certain Roman Catholic societies.

complementary filiation The term for obligations towards kin on the opposite side of the family from which he or she traces descent.

compound family A family characterised by a central figure (typically a powerful man), his or her spouses, sometimes concubines, and all their children. Common in West Africa.

complex structure According to Claude Lévi-Strauss, a kinship systems based on rules about whom one may not marry (e.g., that marriage between close relatives is forbidden). The opposite is an 'elementary structure'.

critique A well-argued criticism.

cross-cousins The children of a brother and a sister. In many societies, cross-cousins are marriageable whereas parallel cousins are not.

cross-cultural Taking into account the understandings of more than one culture.

'Crow' terminology A type of kinship terminology in which the father's sister's daughter is called by the same term as the father's sister, or more generally one in which ego calls several members of his or her father's matrilineal kin group by the same term.

Crow-Omaha systems Claude Lévi-Strauss's term for systems lying in-between elementary and complex ones: systems with 'Crow' or 'Omaha' terminologies in which all those called by kin terms are forbidden as possible spouses.

cultural anthropology Another term for social anthropology, common especially in North America.

cultural ecology The study of relations between culture and the natural world, especially in the theoretical perspective of Julian Steward (see also 'ecology').

cultural materialism The theoretical perspective of Marvin Harris, who argues that there is a direct causal relation between material forces and aspects of culture.

cultural universal A feature found in all cultures. Marriage and the family are often cited as examples. A near synonym is 'human universal'.

culture The totality of ideas, skills and objects shared by a community or society.

'culture and personality' The perspective which emphasizes the 'personality' of whole cultures rather than individuals.

culture circle A cluster of related culture traits, or the geographical area where these are found. The idea was fundamental to German-Austrian diffusionists.

delayed restricted exchange Claude Lévi-Strauss's term for a type of marital exchange between kin groups where women move in one direction in one generation, and in the opposite direction in the next. It is a logical consequence of men marrying fathers' sisters' daughters.

descent theory In kinship, the perspective which involves the study of group structure and rules of residence. Descent theorists are interested in clans, lineages and other kin groups.

development In the usage relevant in anthropology, the planned improvement in the quality of life for disadvantaged communities.

diachronic Though time. Studies which emphasize historical change are diachronic (as opposed to synchronic).

diffusionism The perspective which emphasizes the passing of culture from one community or society to another.

direct exchange Another term for 'restricted exchange'.

discourse In anthropology, the term often means not just a way of talking or writing but one that implies special knowledge or relations of power.

double descent Descent in both the male line and the female line. Everyone belongs to two lineages, one patrilineal and one matrilineal. This is the opposite of cognatic descent.

ecology The study of relations between an organism and its environment. Cultural ecology is the study of ecological relations in the context of human cultures, that is, the relation between a people and their environment.

ego In kinship, the person from whom the relationship is traced. It is from the Latin, meaning 'I' or 'myself'.

elementary structures According to Claude Lévi-Strauss, a kinship system based on categories between which marriage is prescribed (e.g., the category of the cross-cousin). The opposite is a 'complex structure'.

emic Relating to a culture-specific system of thought based on indigenous definitions. Contrast 'etic'.

'Eskimo' terminology A type of kinship terminology in which cousins are distinguished from siblings but there is no distinction between parallel and cross-cousins. The English system is of this type.

ethnicity A person's cultural identity formed on the basis of race, religion, language or national origin.

ethnocentrism Erroneously assuming that another culture is like one's own.

ethnography Literally, 'writing about peoples'. The term refers either to the practice of anthropological fieldwork or the writing-up of the findings of such fieldwork.

ethnographic present The practice of using the present tense in an ethnographic description. It implies a timeless state, with changes since the time of fieldwork not taken into account.

etic Relating to categories held to be universal or based on an outside observer's objective understanding. Contrast 'emic'.

evolution A progression from simple to complex. Usually this change is regarded as gradual.

evolutionism Any perspective which stresses evolution, change for the better or advancement.

family A social unit normally consisting of closely-related people. There are various types of family, but it has been argued that families are found universally as the basis of all societies.

feminism The movement which developed to counteract male dominance and male-dominant understandings of culture and society.

fetishism The belief in fetishes, or objects believed to have supernatural power.

formalism In economic anthropology, the perspective which sees economic systems as all following the same laws of economics, regardless of culture.

'four fields' approach Anthropology as having four branches: social or cultural anthropology, anthropological linguistics, prehistoric archaeology, and biological or physical anthropology. This is the norm in North America but is less common elsewhere.

function A term variously used to denote the purpose of a custom social institution in the abstract, or its relation to other customs or social institutions within a social system.

functionalism Any perspective which emphasizes the functions of customs or social institutions. In anthropology, it refers especially to the perspectives of either Bronislaw Malinowski (regarded as a 'purer' functionalist) or A.R. Radcliffe-Brown (a structural-functionalist).

gender In anthropology, the social and cultural distinctions related to being male or female. In a sense it stands in opposition to 'sex', which describes the biological distinctions.

generalised exchange Claude Lévi-Strauss's term for a type of marital exchange between kin groups where 'exchanges' of women are in one direction only, for example where a son may marry into the same kin group as his father but a daughter may not. It is a logical consequence of men marrying mothers' brothers' daughters.

genitor A child's culturally-recognised biological father.

globalization The processes of increasing social contact and cultural uniformity around the world.

'Hawaiian' terminology A type of kinship terminology in which there is no distinction between siblings and cousins.

horticulture The practice of keeping small vegetable gardens, as opposed to large scale agriculture.

human universal A feature which is the same for all humanity, regardless of culture. A near synonym is 'cultural universal'.

incest taboo The prohibition of sex with a category of person. The range of the taboo varies greatly from society to society, but the fact of it is universal.

indigenous Of local origin.

interpretivism A perspective which emphasizes the interpretation of culture over the quest for formal structures. Clifford Geertz's anthropology is the clearest example, while some of E.E. Evans-Pritchard's work is loosely interpretivist.

'Iroquois' terminology A type of kinship terminology in which cross-cousins are distinguished from parallel cousins. Often parallel cousins are classed together with siblings.

joint family A family in which brothers and their wives and children all live together; an effective form of family structure when brothers share property in common, as in parts of India, China and Africa.

kibbutzim Agricultural communities in Israel in which children are raised collectively.

life cycle The pattern of life from birth to death.

liminality The transitional phase or characteristic reversal associated with it in a rite of passage. For example, when men act as if they are women or old people act as children.

lineage A patrilineal or matrilineal kin group tracing descent from a common ancestor. Members of a lineage will know their relationship to every other member of the lineage (contrast 'clan').

marriage Usually, a relationship between a man and a woman which forms a permanent bond and basis for the family and the legitimation of children. However, anthropologists have shown that there can be a variety of forms of marriage, and the universality of the concept has been called into question.

Marxism Referring to the ideas of Karl Marx. In anthropology, the term implies a theoretical interest in the connections between material forces and relations of power but not necessarily adherence to Marx's political ideology.

mater A child's social mother (including adoptive mother).

matrilineal descent Descent through women, from mother to child, etc.

mode of production In Marxist theory, the combination of the means of production (how people make a living) and relations of production (the ways in which production is organized).

money Any commodity of universal value within a particular society or community (for example, dollars, pounds, beans, shells, gold).

monogamy Marriage to only one other person.

monotheism Belief in one god.

multicultural Having more than one culture in the same society, or an activity which takes account of this fact (like multicultural education).

multilinear evolutionists Those who held that evolution is different from place to place, often because of local environmental influences.

nature In anthropology, often taken to mean the opposite of culture: the natural world as opposed to the cultural and social world.

'Omaha' terminology A type of kinship terminology in which the mother's brother's son is called by the same term as the mother's brother, or more generally one in which ego calls several members of his or her mother's patrilineal kin group by the same term.

parallel cousins The children of two brothers or two sisters. In many societies parallel cousins are treated as brothers and sisters and sharply distinguished from cross-cousins.

participant observation The fieldwork methodology in which the ethnographer learns through both observation and participation in the social life of the people under study.

pastoralism The practice of keeping livestock.

pater A child's social father (including adoptive father).

patrilineal descent Descent through men, from father to child, etc.

polygamy Marriage to more than one other person.

polygyny Marriage between one man and more than one woman; common in several parts of the world, notably in traditional African societies.

polyandry Marriage between one woman and more than one man, usually a group of brothers; the best-known cases are in South Asia, such as the Todas of India, though the custom is dying out.

polytheism Belief in more than one god.

postmodernism The rejection of 'modernist' claims that culture or society can be explained through grand theoretical perspectives. Postmodernists also reject the idea that knowledge is the same everywhere (compare 'relativism').

potlatch A ceremony performed by peoples of the North West Coast of North America. They involve feasting and giving away goods. Giving away goods gains prestige for the giver.

profane Emile Durkheim's term for the ordinary, or what is not sacred.

psychic unity The idea that all humankind shares the same deep understanding of the world.

reflexivity The practice of an ethnographer reflecting on his or her own position in relation to other people during fieldwork.

relativism A perspective which opposes the idea that there are universal values, the same in all cultures. Relativists emphasize the variety of cultures. Postmodernism is an extreme and recent form of this perspective.

restricted exchange Claude Lévi-Strauss's term for a type of marital exchange between kin groups where exchanges of women may go in either direction. It is a logical consequence of men exchanging sisters with each other or marrying women of a category which includes both mothers' brothers' daughters and fathers' sisters' daughters.

rites of passage Rituals to mark the transition from one stage of life to another (such as adolescence to adulthood).

sacred Emile Durkheim's term for what is set apart from the normal world, often including forbidden knowledge or practices and ritual activities. The opposite is 'profane'.

shaman A ritual specialist, especially in the Arctic or the Americas, who mediates between the ordinary world and the spirit world through trance, out-of-body travel, etc.

shamanism The practice of or belief in mediation between the ordinary world and the spirit world by a shaman.

sibling Brother or sister.

social anthropology The study of society in cross-cultural perspective, or more broadly the study of human social life.

social institution An element of a social system (e.g., marriage is an aspect of the kinship system).

social organisation The dynamic aspect of social structure, that is, the activities people engage in as part of the social structure.

social processes A general term employed for cyclical changes in society or changes in society over time.

social stratification The division of society 'vertically' into social classes, castes (as in India), etc.

social structure The elements of society in relation to one another, or the social positions people occupy.

social system A term referring either to specific systems within society (economics, politics, kinship, religion) or to the society as a whole in its systematic aspects.

society A social unit equivalent variously to a language group, a cultural isolate, or a nation state. Also the social relations which exist between members of such a unit.

sociobiologists Scientists who hold that human social evolution is similar to that of animals.

sorcery A learned magical practice whereby an individual performs activities which may be harmful to others.

sphere of exchange A category of items (such as Trobriand kula valuables) which can be exchanged for each other but not normally for other things.

state The highest level of political authority in a society, and that which has the legal power of coercion over its citizens.

structural-functionalism Referring to the ideas of A.R. Radcliffe-Brown, who emphasized functional relations between social institutions.

structuralism Any perspective which emphasizes structural relations as a key to understanding. For structuralists, things acquire meaning through their place in a structure or system. In anthropology, it is the perspective identified most closely with Claude Lévi-Strauss.

subsistence, means of A method of obtaining a living from the environment, for example by hunting, gathering, fishing, herding livestock, or agriculture.

substantivism In economic anthropology, the perspective which sees economic systems as diverse, with economic activity embedded in culture.

'Sudanese' terminology A type of kinship terminology in which ego calls each of his or her cousins by a distinct term: father's sister's son, father's sister's daughter, etc. There will be no generic word like English 'cousin'.

synchronic In the same time period. Studies which concentrate on the present are synchronic (as opposed to diachronic).

taboo A practice which is forbidden, such as incest or cannibalism (in all societies), eating meat (in vegetarian societies), etc.

taxonomy Classification.

technology The knowledge of arts and skills needed to make tools and other useful objects.

theory In science or social science, any perspective or statement which leads to some conclusion about the world. Anthropological theory is centrally concerned with making sense of ethnography and with generalizations about culture or society.

thick description Clifford Geertz's notion of good ethnography as consisting of a multiplicity of detailed and varied interpretations (both the ethnographer's and those of the people under study).

Third World The parts of the world which are less technologically advanced, generally including much of Africa,

Asia and Latin America. The term survives from an old
distinction between First (advanced capitalist), Second (the
former Soviet Block) and Third Worlds.

totem In Ojibwa belief, the spirit of a patrilineal clan represented
by an animal. By extension, a similar spirit among any people.

totemism Any belief system which entails the symbolic
representation of the social (e.g., clan membership) by the
natural (e.g., animal species and their characteristics).

translation analogy The idea that doing ethnography is like
translating a language. The ethnographer learns the local
customs and 'translates' them for people in another culture.

unilinear evolutionists Those who held that there is a precise
line of evolution, the same everywhere.

universal evolutionists Those who hold that only general trends
are the same everywhere.

uxorilocal residence Residence in the locality of the wife.

virolocal residence Residence in the locality of the husband.

witchcraft A magical practice whereby an individual performs
activities which may be harmful to others. Anthropologists
usually use this term to refer specifically to such practices
when the propensity to perform them is believed to be
inherited (as opposed to sorcery, in which they are learned).

Further Reading and Reference

Mention is made of many specific ethnographies and important books in the main text of this book. Below is a selection of recent, general books covering social anthropology and major branches of the subject.

Barfield, Thomas (ed.). *The Dictionary of Anthropology.* Blackwell, 1997. A concise reference book with some excellent entries.

Barnard, Alan. *History and Theory in Anthropology.* Cambridge University Press, 2000. An overview of anthropological theory, with an emphasis on the history of the subject.

Barnard, Alan and Jonathan Spencer (eds.). *Encyclopedia of Social and Cultural Anthropology.* Routledge, 1996. A comprehensive and affordable one-volume encyclopedia.

Borofsky, Robert (ed.). *Assessing Cultural Anthropology.* McGraw Hill, 1994. A highly readable collection of contemporary essays.

Bowie, Fiona. *The Anthropology of Religion: An Introduction* (2nd edition). Blackwell, 2005. A student-friendly book, focused on key ideas and contemporary ethnography.

Coleman, Simon and Bob Simpson (eds.). *Discovering Anthropology: A Resource Guide for Teachers and Students* (5th edition). Royal Anthropological Institute, 1998. A detailed guide, with useful addresses and information on UK anthropology departments and societies.

Davis, John. *Exchange.* Open University Press, 1992. A short, thought-provoking guide to exchange in different societies.

Helman, Cecil G. *Culture, Health and Illness* (4th edition). Butterworth-Heinemann, 2001. An excellent guide to medical anthropology.

Holy, Ladislav. *Anthropological Perspectives on Kinship.* Pluto Press, 1996. An excellent introduction to kinship, especially descent theory.

Ingold, Tim (ed.). *Companion Encyclopedia of Anthropology: Humanity, Culture and Social Life.* Routledge, 1994. A valuable collection of essays by leading anthropologists.

Ingold, Tim (ed.). *Key Debates in Anthropology.* Routledge, 1996. Transcriptions of debates held in Manchester every year between leading anthropologists.

Kuper, Adam. *Anthropology and Anthropologists: The Modern British School* (3rd edition). Routledge, 1996. A highly readable history of modern British social anthropology.

Kuper, Adam and Jessica Kuper (eds.). *The Social Science Encyclopedia* (3rd edition). Routledge, 2004. An important two-volume reference work with lots of entries on anthropology.

Layton, Robert. *An Introduction to Theory in Anthropology.* Cambridge University Press, 1997. A good introduction to anthropological theory, with an emphasis on recent debates.

Lewellen, Ted C. *Political Anthropology* (3rd edition). Praeger Publishers, 2003. A comprehensive overview.

Nolan, Riall. *Development Anthropology.* Westview Press, 1999. A good introduction to the field.

Parkin, Robert. *Kinship: An Introduction to the Basic Concepts.* Blackwell, 1997. A good introduction to kinship, especially alliance theory.

Thin, Neil. *Social Progress and Sustainable Development.* ITDG Publishing, 2002. A very good introduction to the anthropology of development.

Wilk, Richard R. *Economics and Cultures: Foundations of Economic Anthropology.* Westview Press, 1996. An advanced but very readable introduction to applied anthropology.

Useful Websites

A great many websites are devoted to social anthropology. Below are just a few of the most useful, including those with extensive links to help obtain other material. They can help you locate such things as: degree programmes, courses and reading lists, information for teachers and students, and bibliographical resources.

American Anthropological Association
http://www.aaanet.org
Contains details of publications of the AAA and of numerous anthropology resources on the Internet

Anthropological Index
http://aio.anthropology.org.uk/aio/AIO.html
An extremely valuable and easy-to-use bibliographical search engine. Locates articles in all journals held in the Museum of Mankind Library (1950s to the present)

Anthropology Resources on the Internet
http://www.anthropologie.net
Extremely rich; information on books, anthropology departments, Web directories, teaching materials, etc.

The Association of Social Anthropologists
http://www.theasa.org/
The ASA is the main professional association for anthropologists in the UK; the website is mainly for professionals, but also has useful information for students and teachers

European Association of Social Anthropologists
http://www.easaonline.org/
Mainly of interest to professional anthropologists, but also has details of the association's publications and useful links

Institute of Social and Cultural Anthropology (Oxford)
http://www.bodley.ox.ac.uk/external/isca/anthres.html
Maintained by Oxford University, this is a very comprehensive website offering information and links to resources worldwide

National Network for Teaching and Learning Anthropology
http://lucy.ukc.ac.uk/NNTLA/
Maintained by the University of Kent at Canterbury, this website has information of interest to teachers, lecturers and students

The Royal Anthropological Institute of Great Britain and Ireland
http://www.therai.org.uk/
One of the most important anthropological organizations in the world, the RAI sponsors two journals and many events in London and elsewhere

Theory in Anthropology
http://www.indiana.edu/~wanthro/theory.htm
Maintained by Indiana University; takes 'theory' in a broad sense and includes a wide variety of interests: urban, legal, applied, feminist, psychological and ecological anthropology, etc.

Index